Transforming Educational Leadership

Sanaz—

With deep admiration for your vision and storytelling — helping ideas like these find their kinfolk! Talk soon,

Transforming Educational Leadership

Non-Traditional Narratives to Promote Equity in Uncertain Times

Anindya Kundu

OXFORD
UNIVERSITY PRESS

Oxford University Press is a department of the University of Oxford.
It furthers the University's objective of excellence in research, scholarship,
and education by publishing worldwide. Oxford is a registered trade mark of
Oxford University Press in the UK and in certain other countries.

Published in the United States of America by Oxford University Press
198 Madison Avenue, New York, NY 10016, United States of America.

© Oxford University Press 2025

All rights reserved. No part of this publication may be reproduced, stored in a retrieval system,
transmitted, used for text and data mining, or used for training artificial intelligence, in any form or
by any means, without the prior permission in writing of Oxford University Press, or as expressly
permitted by law, by license or under terms agreed with the appropriate reprographics rights
organization. Inquiries concerning reproduction outside the scope of the above should be sent
to the Rights Department, Oxford University Press, at the address above.

You must not circulate this work in any other form
and you must impose this same condition on any acquirer.

CIP data is on file at the Library of Congress.

ISBN 9780197750551

ISBN 9780197750544 (hbk.)

DOI: 10.1093/9780197750582.001.0001

Paperback Printed by Integrated Books International, United States of America

Hardback Printed by Bridgeport National Bindery, Inc., United States of America

The manufacturer's authorized representative in the EU for product safety is
Oxford University Press España S.A., Parque Empresarial San Fernando de Henares,
Avenida de Castilla, 2 – 28830 Madrid (www.oup.es/en or product.safety@oup.com).
OUP España S.A. also acts as importer into Spain of products made by the manufacturer.

The manufacturer's authorised representative in the EU for product safety is Oxford University Press España S.A. of El Parque Empresarial
San Fernando de Henares, Avenida de Castilla, 2 – 28830 Madrid (www.oup.es/en or product.safety@oup.com). OUP España S.A. also acts as
importer into Spain of products made by the manufacturer.

To Ma, Baba, and Didi—my first educators

FOREWORD

PRUDENCE L. CARTER
PROFESSOR OR SOCIOLOGY, BROWN UNIVERSITY
FORMER PRESIDENT OF THE AMERICAN
SOCIOLOGICAL ASSOCIATION

Education Can Save Our Democracy Through Transformative, Equity-Oriented Leadership

The US educational system presents a paradox. On the one hand, it is celebrated globally for its graduates' creativity, innovation, and productivity. On the other hand, it is one of the most effective reproducers of social and economic inequality among its society's members. Many have documented how stratification and other systemic barriers in the US perpetuate educational inequities, particularly for individuals and groups historically excluded from equal opportunities. As educational researchers and social scientists, we continue to ask why this persists. I believe the system will remain unable to uplift all learners, especially those from marginalized and low-income backgrounds, unless we address its underlying cultural logic regarding the fundamental purposes of education. Specifically, we must critically examine an education system that prioritizes individualism and consequentially foments divisions based on social differences such as race, class, language, and immigration status. How to address these challenges are central questions explored by Anindya Kundu as he guides readers through remarkable stories of educational leaders challenging the status quo to promote equity.

Historically, education in the US has evolved through various phases with differing goals. In the mid-nineteenth century, early reformers like Horace Mann and Henry Barnard championed the common schools movement, advocating for mass education to instill democratic values and national identity in (male) students. Their vision centered on the idea of education for the common good and societal benefit. However, this movement was fraught with exclusion and discrimination. Schools, designed to transmit civic and cultural values rooted in traditional Christian and Protestant beliefs, deliberately excluded Indigenous peoples, enslaved and formerly enslaved individuals of African descent, women, and others who were not white and male.

Schooling's purpose evolved in the early twentieth century, especially with the rise in immigration, migration, and industrialization. Its focus became more centered on ideals about how schools should be organized and how to expand literacy and numeracy skills, along with other vocational competencies, to provide a modern economy with an educated citizenry. The public-good nature of education's purpose still prevailed, although less so for political reasons and more for economic ones.

As time and US society progressed, education's purpose evolved to focus on opportunity and proper schooling as a resource for social mobility. In the 1960s and 1970s, the civil rights movement and activists pushed US democracy to grow into a relatively more inclusive society. That included the principle of integration and equal educational opportunity. Charles Hamilton Houston, Thurgood Marshall, and other legal minds, with the assistance of various plaintiffs, sued multiple school districts and the US government for equal educational opportunity and access of Black and other historically excluded groups. Nevertheless, substantial lack of political will and resistance to social integration in schools, equitable funding, deeper support for teacher training, recruitment, pay, and development have mitigated schools' ability to neutralize the depressing effects of child poverty and other resource limitations affecting student well-being. Opportunity gaps (in resources) drive achievement gaps, as Kundu (and others) persuasively argue.

Education's ability to hold society together as a collective with the inclusion of *all* of its people has not yet materialized fully as a national objective. Instead, the demands for individual choices and aspirations have managed to counteract the needs to uphold a multicultural, multiracial democracy. The conflict of *education-as-a-private good* and *education-for-public good* is both political and social. We can see it clearly in a 2019 Pew Research Center poll.[1] Slightly more than a third of whites favor racially mixed schools as opposed to local ones in their communities, which are marked heavily by racial and socioeconomic segregation. The opposite is true for Black Americans, among whom 68% prefer racially and ethnically diverse schools. Latinos and Asians are split down the middle with half of each group favoring diverse schools. Political identity drives a good deal of this: less than 25% of Republicans prefer diverse schools to local ones, while nearly 60% of Democrats do.

From years of research in US schools and personal experience, I know that we don't need integrated schools to "save" Asian, Black, Indigenous, or Latinx students.[2] But, we just might need them to save us from ourselves. Pushback and reversal in society's advancement—what I call the "tipping point of tolerance"—have been intense. While education's purpose hasn't been reimagined beyond its instrumental value for individual social mobility and growing human capital for personal success, arguably, it has another fundamental goal. We need schools for the development of critical thinking, civic awareness, and social cohesion, especially in these times of increased social diversification and the ensuing divisions that have occurred because of these differences.

What we do not need, however, is for public and school officials to live in an unrealistic bubble of erasure and the misleading of students about the fullness of US history, including its relationship with its racist and religiously intolerant past. We need educators to teach students to understand the distinction between national values of equality, liberty, and justice and personal opinions and preferences. The former is

---

[1] Juliana Menasce Horowitz, "Americans See Advantages and Challenges in Country's Growing Racial and Ethnic Diversity," Pew Research Center, May 8, 2019, https://www.pewresearch.org/social-trends/2019/05/08/americans-see-advantages-and-challenges-in-countrys-growing-racial-and-ethnic-diversity/.

[2] Prudence L. Carter, *Stubborn Roots: Race, Culture, and Inequality in U.S. and South African Schools* (Oxford University Press, 2012).

for the public good and democracy; the latter accommodates individual liberty and choice. None of this can occur, nonetheless, without the efforts of transformative, equity-minded thinkers and leaders (a concept advanced by leadership expert Carolyn Shields)[3] —several fine portraits of whom Kundu offers here in this book. For example, you will learn about how a single mother fought against a deeply entrenched, racialized school tracking process to advocate for her daughters' education. You will learn about how a school superintendent led a highly sensitive school closures process by prioritizing the amplification of affected community voices and in the process not just decimating the most vulnerable neighborhoods and schools in the district. You will learn how notable scholars and social scientists who have produced community-engaged scholarship conceptualize and develop projects rooted in experiential knowledge and not mere abstract thinking.

I am aware of no other social and cultural institution in our society like education with both the scale, capacity, and power to help cultivate the agency of the nation's populace to act and engage in ways that engender social progress. Now, more than ever, we need education urgently to help save our democracy from deep threats of authoritarianism and fascism. To accomplish that goal, we must act and encourage the development, recruitment, and selection of a strong cadre of transformative, equity-minded leaders in government, schools, and communities. Transformative equity-minded leadership matters to cultivate both agency of the individuals and communities involved *and* to disrupt the structures and practices in schooling that impede our society's aspirations for strong educational outcomes for all. In the following pages, we learn more about how and why.

---

[3] Carolyn M. Shields, *Transformative Leadership in Education* (Routledge, 2017).

CONTENTS

Prologue 1

Introduction: The Many Forms of Educational Leadership 8
    The Ever-Unequal Contexts of Schooling 12
    Education Debt Affects *Everyone* and Alleviating It Requires *Everyone* 19
    Questions and a Definition 21
    Diverse Storytellers 24
    Why Stories Matter 27
    Achievement and Well-Being for All 30
    Individual Agency Is Helping and Being Helped by *Others* 33
    Who Am I Accountable To? 35
    A Charge to My Reader 37
    Overview of Chapters 39

1. The Sociology of Leading Systems Change 41
    Educational Leaders Maintain Our Social Fabric 41
    Functionalist and Conflict Perspectives Inform Grounded Leadership 47
    The Structure-Agency Dichotomy Meets Debra's Kindergarten Classroom Library 58

Fostering Agency and Mobilizing Forms of Capital
as a Guiding Theoretical Framework   62
Collective Efficacy: A Pivotal Source of Support and Metric of
Collaboration   66
Chapter Summary   69

2. Build Better Systems: Address Students' and Stakeholders' Basic
Needs   70
Saving Starfish: How the Impact of Individual Support Adds Up   71
Safe, but Stretched: Ripple Effects of Relationship-Based Support   75
The Perfect Storm and a Yellow Sweater: Prioritizing Unity in Times
of Crisis   78
"It Was Possible to Do Both": Offering High Expectations and High
Support   82
Chapter Summary   85

3. Make Sense of the Nonsensical: Apply Research to Unearth and
Solve Injustices   90
It Requires Naming It: Racial Inequity as a Symptom of Greater
Forces   91
Fix Something Unfair? That's What I Do All Day: Follow the Trail of
Facts   95
Closing Schools . . . Equitably: Making Tough Decisions Where
Everyone Is Heard   98
There's Room at the Table for All of Us: Inclusion through
Community-Engaged Scientific Inquiry   101
Chapter Summary   106

4. Stick to Your Guns: Lead with Values, Conviction, and
Information   111
with Jason Le-Reselosa
Soul Searching: Finding Solace in Changing Perspectives and Ruffling
Feathers   113

Wrongly Convicted and yet Unwavering in Conviction: The Pursuit of Justice   117

Stepping Down to Take a Stand: Resignation as an Act of Resistance and Disruption   120

Asian Enough: Liberating Identity Through Mental Health Advocacy   124

History Will *Not* Repeat Itself: A Mother's Advocacy   127

Chapter Summary   131

5. Hand-Ups Over Handouts: Promote Agency Above All Else   135
   with Gabriella Portela

   We Have to Look Out for Each Other: Crisis Requires Community   137

   Reducing and Removing Barriers to Make Way for Capable People   140

   Jan's Dream: Create a Lasting Legacy by Fostering Belonging   143

   From Adversity to Advocacy: Mentorship for Lasting Change   146

   Tailored Resources Are the Seeds That Spark Community Empowerment   148

   Chapter Summary   151

6. Center Human Dignity: Champion All People's Right to Receive a Transformative Education   155

   Testifying for Good: Applying One's Influence to Give Greater Platform to Others   156

   For the Love of Books: Promoting Literacy (and Lifelong Education) as a Human Right   160

   The Mother of All: The Only Option Is Love   163

   Obedience Will Only Get You So Far: Social Justice as an Insurgent and Imperative Approach   165

   Nothing to Lose: The Institution Is More Afraid Than You Are   168

Choosing Wellness Over Achievement Cures
the Crisis of Courage   172
Chapter Summary   175

Conclusion   178

The Educational Leadership for Equity Toolkit   *183*
Acknowledgments   *191*
Index   *193*

PROLOGUE

A Concerned Mom Scratches the Surface of a Deeply Rooted Problem

In January 2020, right before the pandemic altered our earth's tilt, I received a message from a woman named Denise Williamson. She had seen my recent TED Talk and something about the talk had left her eager to speak with me.

It was actually my second TED Talk, for which I was less nervous than the first time around. I saw the opportunity as my chance to retake the circular red carpet and speak a greater truth to power: our schools and our school systems *perpetuate* inequality instead of combat it, and we can and must correct course for the betterment of all.

What we need, I said, is a more well-rounded, all-hands-on-deck educational system to break cycles of oppression that leave so many students down and out. I also made the case that supporting marginalized communities actually *strengthens* our economy and civil society. I gave the example of some parents being criminalized for misrepresenting their addresses in order to get better schools for their children, but other parents bribing their children's way into the Ivy Leagues, with few or less severe repercussions.[1]

---

[1] Evan Gerstmann, "The Irony of the Elite College Admissions Bribery Scandal," *Forbes*, March 13, 2019, https://www.forbes.com/sites/evangerstmann/2019/03/13/the-irony-of-the-elite-college-admission-bribery-scandal/?sh=4f31cfc91ce5; Linda Jacobson, "Report: In 24 States, Using False Address to Get Into a Better School Is a

My public engagement with failed promises in education has shown me that the subject resonates differently among different people. Many people hold more "neoliberal" (instead of egalitarian) views in education, which are primarily that a free-market and competition-based education system is fair and necessary to a functioning, capitalist society. My research has led me to believe, and in my talk I argued, that our schools are the *one* place we must be more socially minded; I am convinced that our free-market system has in fact led to individuals only working to enrich themselves without attention to the well-being of others and to the detriment of a society that works for all.

One result, as I see it, is a wealth-based public education system with vastly disparate resources between rich and poor schools. When the kids who desperately rely on free school meals also go to schools with the most drastically underfunded or nonexistent arts programs, least experienced teachers, and most obsolete technology and equipment—places devoid of joy... that's not exactly fair competition, is it?

To me, being able to predict a child's future by their zip code is the central moral issue in our democracy.

My talk, "Closing the 'Opportunity Gap' in US Public Education," became the fifth most popular TED Talk in 2020.[2] Somehow, I found myself on a graphic with Bill Gates. With that exposure came comments, concerns, and questions from folks interested in joining the conversation. At times, fielding messages can be exhausting or disheartening when the sender only shares criticism. My mission has been to champion greater collective responsibilities and accountability in education for the sake of all children. Some have interpreted this to mean that I don't care for individual responsibility, talent, and effort in determining success or again, that I am against healthy competition.

Crime," *The 74*, August 8, 2023, https://www.the74million.org/article/report-in-24-states-using-false-address-to-get-into-a-better-school-is-a-crime/.

[2] The Most Popular Talks of 2020: https://www.ted.com/playlists/780/the_most_popular_talks_of_2020 (accessed April 23, 2025).

Some part of my remarks struck a chord with Denise,[3] a parent of two Black girls. After watching the video, she went straight from TED.com to my personal website and left this brief message on my Contact Me page:

> Would you please call me? . . . I am a minority and an only parent of two school-aged kids. I want to verbalize my comments to your recent TED Talk on closing the achievement gap. As you indicate, access to opportunity is low and I am busy working full-time and raising children. I don't have time to communicate via comment pages. Thanks, Denise.

As anyone who has shared a talk, article, or even TikTok video with the internet knows, the comment section can be brutal, no matter the position you take. I've received countless communications from people telling me that I haven't considered X, Y, or Z influence, or that I'm flatly wrong. I try to remind myself that touching these nerves might indicate that I'm scratching the surface of a broken system—or as we discuss in this book, that challenging the status quo inevitably leads to ruffled feathers.

Sometimes people have reached out to say that they were grateful for my efforts or learned something useful from the evidence or stories I shared. Most of the time exchanges stay on the internet and do not get as intimate as a phone call. Unsure of which camp Denise fell into, something told me to call her and hear her out.

To this day, I also can't help but chuckle to myself at the last line in her message—that she "does not have time to communicate via comment pages"—which (unintentionally) sounds like she is reprimanding me for not being more accessible to busy people like her. But she was simply stating the truth: between raising her daughters and working full-time, Denise's time *was* limited. And her taking time out of her day to reach out showed a passion that piqued my curiosity. So I picked up the phone and dialed Denise's number.

---

[3] Due to the sensitive nature of the information shared, "Denise" is an alias chosen by my friend, as are the names used to represent her two daughters throughout this book.

She sounded surprised when I introduced myself, and we both waited in awkward silence for a few seconds. It became evident that Denise hadn't actually believed I would call. She figured she had shipped a futile paragraph into the vast expanses of the internet with no expectation of hearing back from me or anyone else. It didn't help that I called her on a weekday afternoon, but, I thought, *Isn't that what she requested?*

We broke the ice with some pleasantries and ended up chatting for over thirty minutes. Denise slowly opened up and told me her story, which revolved around her two daughters' access to educational opportunities in Indianapolis. Denise was tired from an endless battle for her daughters' educational rights when she came across my speech. Denise's full story is featured in Chapter 4.

For now, the gist is that Denise's daughters experienced racist sorting, and they and other deserving minority students were blocked from overwhelmingly white honors programs. Denise's eldest, Nicole, was told in sixth grade she lacked the "critical thinking skills" to qualify for middle school advanced math and science, even though she had straight As in fifth grade in those same subjects. Not only that, but Nicole's fifth-grade teacher, a US Presidential Teacher of the Year Winner, had recommended her for honors classes in middle school—a request denied without explanation once the girl arrived at her new building.

Denise detailed how she came to notice the ongoing, racial tracking problem and her actions to try and remedy it. Eventually, she got her daughters into the right classes and on an academically challenging track. But the experience left her dispirited and dismayed toward the educational system at large. We kept in touch and months later, Denise sent me a video of an academic honors graduation celebration at the local high school for the top students of each class. In the video, nearly all of the students appeared to be white. Denise wrote, "How can a school be majority-minority demographically, but then have nearly 100% of its most successful students be nonminority?"

I thought about that for some time. To me, the question in Denise's email, as well as the questions surrounding her daughters' tracking experience, reveal an entrenched problem in education. Improving education requires answering those questions. As Prudence Carter mentions in this book's forward, we should also persistently examine how and *why* these inequalities have persisted. Why are our schools, seventy years after *Brown v. Board of Education*, more segregated today? How have these systems become so normalized?

These thoughts compelled me to write this book, to broaden the definition of who is an educational leader to be as inclusive as possible. Through research, I gathered examples of unorthodox leadership at all levels—parents, students, educators, leaders, policymakers, and community members—presenting select vignettes for you in the chapters that follow.

If we don't fight for ourselves, who will? This book tells the stories of stakeholders—some already in leadership positions and some taking the reins for the first time on their own, like Denise—who disrupted inequality and spread awareness of social justice and liberation through their sense of identity and agency.

The majority-minority high school Denise's daughters attended, as well as the larger, overwhelmingly white Indianapolis Public Schools District, might proclaim that being integrated allowed it to vehemently deny instituting explicitly racist tracking. But the phenomenon may still occur without any formal mandates or authorizations.[4] Similarly, many groups serving children—examples of which appear in the stories that follow—would reject the idea that they are *actively* oppressive, unethical, or unfair. And they very well may not be, *knowingly*. Actors who unevenly provide fundamentally necessary resources may even have good intentions, making them a lot more like anti-heroes than actual villains, but thus also harder to challenge.

In the face of these palpable, daunting, and often disguised forces, Denise Williamson stood tall. In her tireless advocacy to challenge the situation her daughters were in, she wrote countless emails and made countless phone calls to the principal, counselors, and teachers at Nicole's new middle school. She secured meetings during the school day, when she had to be excused from work. At these meetings, she

---

[4] Jeannie Oakes, *Keeping Track: How Schools Structure Inequality* (Yale University Press, 2005); Karolyn Tyson, ed., *Integration Interrupted: Tracking, Black Students, and Acting White After Brown* (Oxford University Press, 2011); Amanda E. Lewis and John B. Diamond, *Despite the Best Intentions: How Racial Inequality Thrives in Good Schools* (Oxford University Press, 2024).

repeatedly had to state her rationale for making her request for placing her daughters in the advanced track. Strategically, Denise also kept copies of her correspondence. The middle school staff denied the request for all of Nicole's sixth grade schooling but placed her in advanced courses in seventh grade, saying that her previous exclusion had been an "oversight." Nicole continued to thrive, and so did her sister.

Despite her daughters' success, Denise lamented that her painstaking efforts were not likely to create lasting and systemic changes for other deserving students. The only parent who reached out to learn from Denise's efforts to help her own child access honors was white. Still, it felt good to vent, Denise told me with palpable regret.

After we hung up, I found myself ruminating. Denise's efforts deserved to be chronicled—to be commemorated to inspire others. I thought about the other parents who routinely experienced injustices related to their children's education but were without the wherewithal, access, or platform to do something about it. Some do not have the time or space to vent.

As an exhausted dad to toddlers, I realize more every day how limited the energy reserves of parents are. The same goes for teachers, school leaders, district leaders, and other professionals who serve children. Those who have the ability to influence policy are all often tired or burned out from pushing what seem to be immovable boulders.

Denise helped me see that advocating for children is not draining but lifegiving. Her story helped me realize that an important aspect of educational leadership was often being ignored: individuals and communities can and must constantly *resist* structural obstacles—those that impede schools from achieving their potential of promoting opportunity for all—to actively promote a more "desegregated" ideal. A desegregated ideal would be one where no student experiences additional barriers due to inherited and arbitrary factors about who they are, where they live, and what their families look like.

Effectively justice-oriented educational leadership implies not simply managing systems in place (and subsequently the status quo), but disrupting them.

Advocates like Denise face the system to change it for good. These folks and their stories are not readily found in the published materials that train educational leaders. This book changes that.

The leaders here share stories of how they made change happen, offering perspectives that can be adapted by anyone—from student to district administrator—in an inequitable school context. Those who have triumphed can help others begin to do the same, building enough momentum to finally push immovable boulders off the path for good.

INTRODUCTION

The Many Forms of Educational Leadership

What Do I Know About Educational Leadership?

Fast forwarding about eighteen months from my call with Denise, I moved to Miami to begin my tenure-track professorship in educational leadership at Florida International University. I had worn other hats in education and industry but this was my first appointment as a full-time faculty member of academia. In my first semester I was assigned to teach a graduate-level course titled "Introduction to Educational Leadership." Even though I'd gained ample experience teaching undergraduate and graduate students while obtaining my PhD at NYU, this course had me slightly apprehensive.

You see, I've always aimed for my work to be applicable to school contexts and educational professionals serving diverse students. I also enjoy working with practitioners who engage in the much more important work of directly serving students. But at the same time, I'm not afraid to admit that my experience *in* schools, outside of researching what works in them, is limited. I am foremost a sociologist. My new students were all full-time teachers looking to advance their career through either a master's or doctoral degree or a school leadership certificate and were on the path to becoming principals, school-based administrators, or district leaders. I wondered how I would be able to speak practical research-based truth to their school-based wisdom. My old friend, Imposter Syndrome, tapped on my shoulder.

Worse, the former instructor of my course handed me a thick textbook that had been the backbone for the course. I was certainly grateful for it, but as I combed through the hundreds of pages of that book and others, I found the different theories, diagrams, figures, and case studies slightly impersonal. The whole text surrounded the idea of *maintaining* and *managing* systems and processes in and around schools to promote student achievement. But sometimes, I thought as I flipped through, don't these systems and processes need to be *disrupted* to serve more students?

The case studies and scenarios felt hypothetical and disconnected from the real goings-on of schools and the realities that professionals in these spaces face. Complex educational ecosystems were distilled into business-like components. I searched for inspiration. I asked, *Is this sufficient to prepare educational leaders for the kinds of challenges they will undoubtedly face?*

In fairness, the textbooks do a solid job of priming students for the Florida Educational Leadership Exam (FELE) and other standardized tests across the country, which many of my students planned to take. However, in terms of preparing individuals to lead transformational change; motivate stakeholders, staff, and community members; and build momentum for advocating for the achievement of *all* students, I felt that there was a need for real stories that aspiring leaders could learn from.

During sleepless nights leading up to my first day of teaching, fundamental questions gnawed at me: What is educational leadership and what does it look like, given the worsening conditions of public schools and the fleeing of teachers from the profession? Can anyone be an educational leader? What precisely makes the leadership educational? Do people get to learn something in the process? What traits and strategies result in the serving of all students and mobilizing others around that same mission?

I structured my syllabus around answering these questions. I wanted to offer a course where my practical research experience and learnings could work synergistically with the real-world knowledge of my practitioner students and the more formal materials they needed. When the term began, my students were excited to convene with and learn from other hopeful leaders across their school system.

My initial literature review of leadership scholarship along these veins—work which examines how community members from marginalized vantage points can usher in needed democratic reform—provided me some groundwork upon which to stand. I came across scholars with unique perspectives on leadership, including but not limited to, Jean Anyon (a critical theorist who examined social movements and activism); Dana Mitra (a proponent of student voice), Michael O'Malley, Jennifer Sandlin, and Jake Burdick (champions of a more public pedagogy to dismantle oppressive hegemonic and institutional forces); and Carolyn Shields (who calls for transformative leadership to specifically promote social justice). I also discovered rising newcomers bringing important perspectives to the field, including but certainly not limited to Liane Hypolite, Andrene Castro, and Darrius Stanley, who brought an urgency to their research, not shying from applying critical race perspectives to understanding important questions from how to build sustainable community-engaged partnerships and teacher recruitment and retention pipelines. I felt reinspired immersing myself into writing which positioned equity and inclusion as must-haves, not simply nice-to-haves.

Through blending theory and practice in their research, these scholars demonstrated that justice was not an ambiguous ideal but rather a concrete and realizable opportunity. There was an increasingly established lane within the field to travel upon.

In addition to examining research literature, throughout the semester we studied and presented examples of leaders who had motivated us and summoned us to be our best selves. We told horror stories that we had either heard or directly experienced about leaders who created unnecessary conflict, tension, or disengagement through their approaches, personalities, or style. I hosted guest speakers from around the country, including some whose stories I present in this book, who shared their knowledge on which leadership practices do and do not work.

We had more specific discussions, too. We talked about how to create community-service oriented schools in a city like Miami, Florida, a traditionally conservative region, where offering students and their families social support like free meals and extended school hours might be called socialism and seen as government overreach. My students told me that those kinds of holistic and wraparound strategies probably came more naturally to a place like New York City than to Miami. Still, we agreed that stakeholder buy-in is critical to implementing policies that meet students' nonacademic needs. We have to treat nonacademic needs as nonnegotiable and hope that the broader public can come to see why.

We asked each other how to create school climates of inclusion and cultural competency, especially when students in a single class might represent the wide-ranging, nonmonolithic, geopolitical diversity of Black and Brown Latinx communities. In those settings, how do we invite students to tell their stories and take pride in the identities that most resonate with them?

That first semester at FIU felt successful because we went well beyond the scope of standard educational leadership texts. I became more convinced that my students were *already* educational leaders because they cared about having these kinds of conversations. If they weren't leaders, they would not have devoted their career to serving young people.

Not only that, my students were steadfast in their relentless pursuit of self-improvement to provide better learning experiences for their students. Like many school professionals across the world, they referred to their students as "*my* students, *my* kids." While this can be seen as a controversial or paternalistic sentiment in some education circles, to me highlights the seriousness and nurturing with which they approach their work. Their passion is similar to that of Denise Williamson's.

To better serve them and other aspiring leaders, I needed to keep learning too. If I wanted to feel worthy of the knighthood of Professor of Educational Leadership, I *needed* to have an unwavering grasp of what educational leadership is—what it looks and feels like at its purest forms. I needed to put research to use for good practice. This book tackles those newly emerging challenges and shows how people have overcome them in real-life situations.

The first seed implanted by meeting Denise Williamson had now germinated through the thoughtfulness and dedication of my first group of students at FIU. It was time to move beyond ideation to action. A goal started coming into focus, one aligned with most of my other work: creating connections and collaboration among the academy, the practitioner, and the public.

The Ever-Unequal Contexts of Schooling

If we wanted to only quickly answer Denise's questions about how these things happen before moving on, we could point to the effect of immediate *biases* in educational contexts, both implicit and explicit, that cause students to be grouped not solely by merit but also by arbitrary factors such as their race, class, and cultural conditioning. Such biases are shared by both the educators and people in power who group the students and then internalized by the students who subsequently make sense of their place in the world through these categorizations. But to offer Denise the explanation she and her daughters *deserve* requires deliberation and interrogation.

Anything less will not identify and repair harmful yet commonplace practices—including racialized tracking. Too often parents and other key stakeholders—especially those in marginalized communities, *not* Moms for Liberty—are provided quick, overgeneralized answers to real concerns, offering them no real avenues to participate fully in their children's education. The result is more community members feeling estranged from and apathetic toward education policy.

Again, my goal is not to imply that underresourced schools are deficient institutions; on the contrary, the only deficiency these needed spaces their professionals have is a lack of support to overcome palpable structural obstacles. My examination of leadership which confronts these barriers is not to promote an individual-centric heroism but rather highlight the collectivist themes and approaches that are needed to promote equity-oriented change.

Karolyn Tyson, in *Integration Interrupted*, and Jeannie Oakes, in *Keeping Track*, both examine how curricular tracking defines the US school system and its outcomes but is largely unquestioned by adults.[1] The hierarchization of students perpetuates schools' "hidden curriculum," or the things that students are not explicitly assessed on but that influence the pedagogies they receive.[2] Children (including Denise's daughters) feel the daily toll of this tracking and these segregated learning environments. Their experiences affect how they view the world and their sense of self-worth.

We all internalize our experiences—what we are taught, told, and notice—from early ages. I'll always remember the time a girl in my kindergarten class handed me a *browner* crayon than the one I was using while drawing self-portraits. I don't remember what she said and I don't believe she had ill will, but she wanted to let me know her opinion that I was darker than I saw myself. (Another time a child told me my skin color was the color of poop, which I would say was meant maliciously.)

Educational systems should recognize and uplift "differenceness" and multiple forms of giftedness to foster each child's self-worth.[3] We must create spaces where students different from one another are fully *integrated* so they are open to notice, identify, and speak on their differences in order to live harmoniously together. Most often, injustices have been brought to light by the people who are kept on the margins of society and must fight for a quality education.[4] Without people's valiant efforts—in questioning exclusion and taking a stand against

---

[1] Karolyn Tyson, *Integration Interrupted: Tracking, Black Students, and Acting White after Brown* (Oxford University Press, 2011); Jeannie Oakes, *Keeping Track: How Schools Structure Inequality* (Yale University Press, 2005).

[2] J. R. Martin, "What Should We Do with a Hidden Curriculum When We Find One?," *Curriculum Inquiry* 6, no. 2 (1976): 135–51; H. A. Giroux and A. N. Penna, "Social Education in the Classroom: The Dynamics of the Hidden Curriculum," *Theory & Research in Social Education* 7, no. 1 (1979): 21–42.

[3] Anindya Kundu, *The Power of Student Agency: Looking Beyond Grit to Close the Opportunity Gap* (Teachers College Press, 2020).

[4] Jarvis R. Givens, *Fugitive Pedagogy: Carter G. Woodson and the Art of Black Teaching* (Harvard University Press, 2021); D. N. Harris and T. R. Sass, "Teacher Training, Teacher Quality and Student Achievement," *Journal of Public Economics* 95 (2011): 798–812; Lisa M. Stulberg, *Race, Schools, and Hope: African Americans and School Choice After Brown* (Teachers College Press, 2008).

such practices—we would never have expanded educational rights to include more people, moving away from an elitist school system toward one that can boast universal access.

The larger question of why race- and class-based inequality remains so prevalent and influential in our educational spaces requires an honest and sociohistorical perspective.

Though de jure, or by law, segregation and overt white supremacy may no longer be present in school policies and regulations, they still exist in more subtle and less explicit forms, such as funding disparities between schools serving students of different socioeconomic backgrounds and representation or nonrepresentation of certain people and cultures in curricula. Also, though currently primarily dormant, white supremacy may be making a comeback. Hate groups like the Proud Boys still exist, and their blatant use of intimidation tactics to flaunt their racist ways in public spaces betoken the continued existence of these hateful beliefs in society, even if they are less overt than they were historically.

Seventy-one years ago (from the year I am writing this), in 1954, the landmark *Brown v. Board of Education* officially struck down the principle of "separate but equal" facilities, but it was wholly ineffective at addressing the force of racism in the United States and the unequal treatment of minority racial groups in our society. The truth is that racism continues to roil our society today, even if people are no longer lynched in public and Jim Crow laws are not as blatantly oppressive as they once were.

A year after *Brown*, Chief Justice Earl Warren wrote in an opinion that local jurisdictions must act with "deliberate speed" to desegregate their constituent school districts. Unironically, it seems that our education system has taken that advice to heart, moving deliberately slower than molasses in achieving racial progress, even backtracking at times.

Not that long ago racism was codified in government policies such as redlining. The government ranked neighborhoods by desirability and home buyers in Black neighborhoods, shown in red on maps, could get only subprime loans. But even after redlining was outlawed and the civil rights movement led to reforms, *racism, classism, sexism,* and other *isms* always found their way around formal rules. White flight, or white families leaving urban neighborhoods or schools predominantly populated by minorities, continues.[5]

In *White Space, Black Hood*, Sheryll Cashin shines a light on how excluding Black Americans from affluent white spaces is a gradual process entailing the deliberate and intentional hoarding of opportunities and privileges, like limited seats in honors programs. There is a spatial logic to inequality: concentrated affluence often means that neighborhoods have been or will become predominantly white as rising costs of goods and services and gradual gentrification displace socially and economically disadvantaged others.

According to Cashin, "The segregation of affluence facilitates opportunity hoarding, whereby the most affluent neighborhoods enjoy the best public services, environmental quality, and private, public, and natural amenities, while all other communities are left with fewer, poorer-quality resources."[6] In other words, the *macro* context of society (i.e., the spatial distribution of race, manipulated through housing access) affects the *micro* context of how people experience each other in society. This can lead white residents, who seldom encounter Black and other minorities, starting to perceive people of other races as less deserving of exceptional schools and social resources. In Miami, from where I write this, there is hypersegregation. Poor areas with higher crime rates are predominantly Black. Wealthier communities (many of which are gated) rarely have any Black residents; from my conversations with people in these areas, I can say I've noticed relationships between residents who maintain prejudiced views toward Black people and their culture

---

[5] Jacob W. Faber, "We Built This: Consequences of New Deal Era Intervention in America's Racial Geography," *American Sociological Review* 85, no. 5 (2020): 739–75; Erica Frankenberg, Jongyeon Ee, Jennifer B. Ayscue, and Gary Orfield, *Harming Our Common Future: America's Segregated Schools 65 Years After Brown* (Civil Rights Project, 2019); Pedro A. Noguera and Esa Syeed, *City Schools and the American Dream 2: The Enduring Promise of Public Education* (Teachers College Press, 2020); Gloria Ladson-Billings, *The Dreamkeepers: Successful Teachers of African American Children*, 2nd ed. (Jossey-Bass, 2009); Pedro A. Noguera, "Schools, Prisons, and Social Implications of Punishment: Rethinking Disciplinary Practices," *Theory into Practice* 42, no. 4 (2003): 341–50.

[6] Sheryll Cashin, *White Space, Black Hood: Opportunity Hoarding and Segregation in the Age of Inequality* (Beacon, 2021), 111.

and these opinion-holders' inexperience around Black people as well as a lack of a more sociohistorical context.

One of my favorite books is *The Sum of Us*, by Heather McGhee, largely because of her brilliant, overarching historical metaphor. Did you know that in the 1950s, throughout the United States, there were large, lavish resort-style public swimming pools spread across big cities? If you didn't, you're not alone! Once a large public investment, these pools have disappeared primarily because white communities in the era of mandated desegregation decided they would rather fill the pools with concrete than desegregate them and allow Black children and families to swim in them.

Think about that for a second: rather than allow everyone to enjoy a public good, people decided no one would have a pool. As McGhee says, "racism drained the pool."[7] I would go one step further and say that racism causes us all to drown.

Sociologist Eve Ewing says that like "an electrical current running through water, race has a way of filling space even as it remains invisible."[8] In the same vein, the sociologists Amanda Lewis and John B. Diamond succinctly depict how racism collides with our lives even today, in school and other environments, in *Despite the Best Intentions*:

> Our racial history is part of our present ... its legacies can be felt in the ways schools are organized, in how neighborhoods are laid out, in the composition of our family trees, in the unconscious stereotypes that get primed when we mentally sort people along racial lines. We walk around with it, and while it is never the only dynamic in the room, it matters ... Our long racial history has resulted in both entrenched material inequalities and entrenched cultural belief systems. In addition to providing ways of making sense of abstract and distant hierarchies, these belief systems also play out in daily interactions. Research in social psychology shows, for example, that these belief systems attach status or value to distinguishing attributes such

---

[7] Heather McGhee, *The Sum of Us: What Racism Costs Everyone and How We Can Prosper Together* (One World, 2021).

[8] Eve Ewing, *Ghosts in the Schoolyard: Racism and School Closings on Chicago's South Side* (University of Chicago Press, 2018), 10.

as race. Resulting race-based status beliefs shape how we understand others and ourselves, how we make sense of the racial landscape in which we operate, and how we act and interact . . . Status beliefs both construct and justify social inequality between categories of people.[9]

Ewing, Lewis, and Diamond paint a picture of how the structures of race and racism exist and shape our modern world, including within the operation of institutions that are charged with promoting equity, especially schools. As educators, we should all understand and wholeheartedly believe that *achievement itself cannot be race-based*, because race has been socially constructed—given and assigned meaning over time without any biological basis.[10] The American linguist Noam Chomsky has one of my favorite assessments on achievement: attributing differences in (student outcomes) to differences between races, is like attributing differences in (student outcomes) to differences between heights.[11] They have no connection.

Some replace race with *culture* as the reason for underachievement. Too often we hear people say things like, *Those kids don't care about their education*. Or, *their parents aren't invested in their education*. In the absence of remarkable parents like Denise—those who would go to the edge of the earth for their children's right to learn—these rationales are justifications for the status quo. Further, the status quo is often upheld by actors—organizations, groups, and institutions, like the school Denise's daughters attended—that mean well but unconsciously promote systems that benefit some students while marginalizing others/

Michael Harrington's prominent thesis on the "culture of poverty" addressed similar conversations on poverty and agency. Harrington was

---

[9] Amanda E. Lewis and John B. Diamond, *Despite the Best Intentions: How Racial Inequality Thrives in Good Schools* (Oxford University Press, 2015), 7; A. E. Lewis and J. B. Diamond, *Despite the Best Intentions: How Racial Inequality Thrives in Good Schools* (Oxford University Press, 2024).

[10] Ewing, *Ghosts in the Schoolyard*; Lewis and Diamond, *Despite the Best Intentions*; Anindya Kundu, *The Power of Student Agency: Looking Beyond Grit to Close the Opportunity Gap* (Teachers College Press, 2020).

[11] Kundu, *The Power of Student Agency*.

the first to describe poverty as both a structure and a byproduct of neglect from multiple institutions and systems (failing schools, poor housing conditions, lack of access to healthcare, lack of jobs). He thoroughly documented how poverty is cyclical and smothering. In the 1960s, however, this message was co-opted by conservative policymakers who latched onto only the tagline in order to fight progressive, anti-poverty legislation, intentionally misinterpreting Harrington to "behavioralize" poverty, sounding the dog whistle on "welfare queens" and layabouts. Applying such tropes to children shows how truly ignorant these ideas are.[12]

Matthew Desmond, in *Poverty, by America*, describes US childhood poverty alleviation after the sweeping social safety legislation Congress passed during the COVID-19 pandemic. The gains were quickly forfeited as public sentiment soured toward relief, in the belief that such policies furthered dependency structures and people's unwillingness to work. The skewed view some take toward culture—quick to paint others as lazy or undeserving—is a massive blockade to social equity and progress for children.[13]

And yet culture, like IQ, is *dynamic*. Culture (and IQ) are shaped by structural forces, experiences, and opportunities. Denying a deserving student entry into an honors program is denying them the opportunity to learn the culture of the honors program. Rather than view culture through a deficit perspective we should strive to realize that the only deficit is "not being afforded a comparable number of experiences and opportunities from which to learn and grow that is afforded to [those with] more privilege."[14]

I define privilege (and relatedly, "underprivilege") as having greater (or less) access than others to opportunity and rewards because of inherited background. Denying the existence of privilege and disadvantage denies the barriers many students must overcome to reach the same outcome—including students holding a job and their immigration status, language proficiency, the safety of their commute to school, and other important factors.

---

[12] Michael Harrington, *The Other America* (Simon & Schuster, 1962).
[13] Matthew Desmond, *Poverty, By America* (Crown, 2023).
[14] Kundu, *The Power of Student Agency*, 30.

Until we learn to account for and balance *privilege*, past and present racist and inequitable policy will continue to reverberate, even if many modern policies are less overtly racist than they were in the past. Privilege brings the past into the present to benefit some at the expense of others.

Perhaps then, even opportunity might be an outdated goal when promoting equitable human development and economic mobility for all. We must not only provide opportunities to those with underprivilege but also lower barriers to entry and persistence for students. Getting a student into college does little unless that student is connected to mentors, resources, and other opportunities that will allow them to persist and excel in higher education and in the workforce. Educational leadership should lower multifaceted, complex barriers, many of which manifest invisibly in unequal schooling contexts—such as the racialized tracking practice Denise noticed—to achieve a vision of education where all students can soar.

Education Debt Affects *Everyone* and Alleviating It Requires *Everyone*

Gloria Ladson-Billings refers to overall disparities in educational access and outcomes as the "education debt." Ladson-Billings's colleague, the economist Robert Haveman, described the debt as accumulating from "the foregone schooling resources that we could have (should have) been investing in (primarily) low-income kids, which deficit leads to a variety of social problems (e.g., crime, low productivity, low wages, low labor force participation) that require on going public investment . . . suck[ing] away resources that could go to reducing the achievement gap."[15] The education debt grows through a negative feedback loop because depriving one generation a quality education is a denial that snowballs through successive generations.

---

[15] Gloria Ladson-Billings, "From the Achievement Gap to the Education Debt: Understanding Achievement in US Schools," *Educational Researcher* 35, no. 7 (2006): 5.

Black and other students of color have always disproportionately attended underresourced schools, which leads to diminished expectations for them.[16] Students in these communities bear the brunt of overpunishment and overpolicing.[17] A student's *first* suspension from school is a key turning point in their life history increasing their odds for repeat incarceration over time.[18] Lower-income students of color have a hand on their backs pushing them into a school-to-prison industrial pipeline instead of a school-to-work pathway to industry. This was true even during the pandemic when learning went virtual and poor kids were at home with inadequate internet connections.

As Amanda Lewis and John Diamond reason in their book *Despite the Best Intentions, integration* has never resembled full-on *desegregation*, although the two are often discussed interchangeable.[19] Integration is the façade which absolves us from confronting the education debt and understanding we have not actively desegregated our schools. Desegregating our schools will benefit all students and lead us toward prosperity and stability for all.

I propose broadening Ladson-Billings's concept of the educational debt. Surely it causes a great void in society (the untapped potential of young people and diminished social relations), and communities with fewer resources and more concentrated structural obstacles feel it more. In natural disasters or pandemics, poorer communities experience more harm and delayed recovery.[20]

I contend that we also all experience educational debt on a *personal* level. Schools are unable to deliver the potential that society promised

---

[16] P. L. Carter and K. G. Welner, eds., *Closing the Opportunity Gap: What America Must Do to Give Every Child an Even Chance* (Oxford University Press, 2013); Jonathan Kozol, *Savage Inequalities: Children in America's Schools* (Harper Perennial, 1991); Sean J. Drake, *Academic Apartheid: Race and the Criminalization of Failure in an American Suburb* (University of California Press, 2022).

[17] Monique Morris, *Pushout: The Criminalization of Black Girls in Schools* (The New Press, 2016.

[18] Paul Hemez, John J. Brent, and Thomas J. Mowen, "Exploring the School-to-Prison Pipeline: How School Suspensions Influence Incarceration During Young Adulthood," *Youth Violence and Juvenile Justice* 18, no. 3 (2019): 235–55.

[19] Lewis and Diamond, *Despite the Best Intentions.*

[20] US Census Bureau, "Income Inequality Linked to Social Vulnerability to Disasters," last modified February 2024, https://www.census.gov/library/stories/2024/02/cre-for-equity.html.

they would—again, because of structural disinvestments—if they are not as (socially, economically, culturally) integrated as they could have been, and we all lose. We feel these debts today as adults and young people in the US continue to have worse mental and physical health outcomes than in other parts of the developed world.[21] We feel these educational debts impacting our overall wellness as well as in our day-to-day realities living in a polarized country—ideologically, culturally, racially, and economically—where it becomes increasingly harder to find common ground with our neighbors.

Our school systems could have the power—if we reinvest in them and reclaim education as a collective responsibility—to reduce the educational debt and cure ailments like bias and injustice. That power is wielded in large part by individuals like Denise, and the brave and tireless educational leaders, teachers, community members, and others who dedicate their lives to the improvement of our educational systems. Many unheralded heroes endeavor to serve all students. They are led by love, bravery, and conviction. They are *leaders* whose stories all deserve a platform to be told.

Questions and a Definition

The main questions I look to answer in this book, through narrative-based research, are the following:

1. What definition of educational leadership adequately captures the different elements behind inspiring the achievement and well-being of *all* students?
2. What are elements of efficient and successful educational leadership, as described and exemplified by those who advocate for education for all?
3. What qualities do successful leaders deem important in enlisting the support of others toward common causes?

---

[21] Agency for Healthcare Research and Quality, "Child and Adolescent Mental Health," in *2022 National Healthcare Quality and Disparities Report*, Agency for Healthcare Research and Quality, October 2022, https://www.ncbi.nlm.nih.gov/books/NBK587174/.

4. How do leaders work around conflict and tensions and manage the morale of their team in disruptive times?
5. When structural-level challenges arise, how do leaders develop strategies to confront them?
6. How can leaders foster their own agency and the agency of others to enact positive change within education and for communities?

Locating a succinct, formal definition for "educational leadership" is harder than you might think. Perhaps this is because within the field most of the critical practices, effective methods, and pillars for excellence are constantly debated and evolving. A set of Professional Standards for Educational Leaders (PSEL) has been adopted by most states, with a less than ironic exception being Florida, which has adopted its own Florida Principal Leadership Standards (FPLS). These standards typically guide school leaders on their responsibilities to stakeholders, but especially students. Hopeful school leaders are tested on this material to demonstrate their competence and potential for being a school or district leader.

I mention these two standards to show there is no absence of thought on what educational leadership entails. Theories on educational leadership and how to improve it abound in the introductions to handbooks and books on school leadership. By the 1950s, qualifications and credentials became more required of US school leaders and the talk around standards, responsibilities, and school operations took hold soon thereafter. Educational leadership has risen to the forefront of studies concerning education and management, and that rise is correlated with an increased global focus on managing complex organizations.[22] I consulted texts frequently cited by other scholars and singularly focused on the concept of educational leadership, what it is, and how to use it effectively. From this I formulated a broad field description: the most fundamental quality of leadership seems to be sustained effort to enact positive change and improve an organization's processes and

---

[22] Nigel Bennett, Christine Wise, Philip A. Woods, and Janet A. Harvey, *Distributed Leadership: A Review of Literature* (National College for School Leadership, 2003).

effectiveness while managing others to share the same goal. In education, maintaining effective leadership is essential to the fair, successful, and harmonious functioning of schools and treatment of people inside them.

Practitioners and scholars of educational leadership generally agree that it is meant to be a shared responsibility and that it is intensely context-specific.[23] This shared responsibility not only includes the professional staff of the school and its programs; it also extends to the service recipients—the students and their communities—and requires their engagement. That is, those leading in education must become familiar with the social, cultural, and political environment they operate within.[24]

Definitions of educational leadership also often specify who can and should lead. Some scholars narrow this category to teachers, principals, administrators, and so on, whereas others argue that we each have the capacity for educational leadership. I align with the latter group.

Many definitions of educational leadership also distinguish it from organizational management, which focuses more on maintaining the status quo; leadership, in contrast, moves forward toward system improvement. For example, a principal of a school would exercise both educational leadership and management. The former may entail brainstorming visions and goals for the school, and the latter enforces policies ensuring the smooth functioning of a school's daily routines.

I developed my own definition of educational leadership. In the chapters that follow, you will see how this definition came to form, but it makes sense to share it upfront here to guide your reading:

> Educational leadership is the intentional, resourceful, and purposeful improvement of educational and school systems, to create positive changes in the lives of students of all backgrounds and ages. It is a practical approach rooted in acknowledging obstacles, testing and

---

[23] Michael Connolly, Chris James, and Michael Fertig, "The Difference Between Educational Management and Educational Leadership and the Importance of Educational Responsibility," *Educational Management Administration & Leadership* 47, no. 4 (2019): 504–19.

[24] Helen O'Sullivan and John West-Burnham, *Leading and Managing Schools* (Sage, 2011).

implementing solutions, harnessing hope, and mobilizing other educational professionals and their strengths toward achieving equitable outcomes. Educational leadership, ultimately, serves each student to the fullest capacity of existing resources to expand opportunity for others.

My definition of educational leadership can be a flexible signpost and reminder for you—whether you are an educational professional, an academic, or anyone with a stake in improving education—that if you are working to improve conditions for students, you are on the right track. The work is not easy, but I believe that when individuals are beckoned by hope rather than meander behind fear or despair, positive outcomes are more likely to result. Hope is also contagious.

Diverse Storytellers

To answer questions 2 through 6, I interviewed a team of amazing students, parents, school and district leaders, thought leaders, and prominent practitioners.[25] In the chapters that follow, they share their stories of identifying general problems that stand in the way of promoting success *for all students*. Their diverse sets of expertise and narratives help me answer the ever-present questions about educational leadership that I raised earlier, as well as some others.

I attempted to include all types of stakeholders including those not typically heard to expand our mental framework of educational leadership. The discourse on who can be a leader and what leadership looks like has broadened. Researchers of educational leadership and leadership education study how students can be leaders of their own educational contexts).

Students, who often have the most fresh, innovative, and certainly relevant perspectives on how we can address age-old problems, have spearheaded change and progress in education. Dana Mitra has explored how youth-adult partnerships in leadership shape educational

---

[25] Graduate students Gabby Portela and Jason Le-Reselosa collaborated with me for the stories featured in Chapters 4 and 5.

practices to be more inclusive.[26] This body of work frames youth voice as a primary component for improving pedagogies and reshaping hierarchies of power, noting that the US lags behind other countries in this.[27]

Students are critical in ushering in democratic reform into schooling spaces.[28] I include a few student voices in this book on educational leadership to inspire others to include students in a more expansive definition of who is an educational leader. Graduate students, not included here, should be thought of as school leaders in development and agents of progressive change. Leadership education programs should encourage graduate students to research existing challenges and practice methods for addressing them.[29]

Like Denise Williamson, parents and guardians have some of the most valuable insights and have ushered in some of the most important advances in educational equity. Scholars have discovered a need for such outside-in reform, finding that grassroots activism counters systems of top-down accountability in education and reorganizes the concentration of power.[30] Yet parents can feel as if they do not belong in conversations on what their kids need. We should also include figures in children's lives beyond biological parenthood, making room for other chosen adults and caretakers. Building collective capacity by partnering with parents, community members, activists, and organizations is especially necessary in urban areas where opportunities and resources are limited.[31]

---

[26] Dana L. Mitra, "Adults Advising Youth: Leading While Getting Out of the Way," *Educational Administration Quarterly* 41, no. 3 (2005): 520–53; Dana Mitra, "Student Voice in Secondary Schools: The Possibility for Deeper Change," *Journal of Educational Administration* 56, no. 5 (2018): 473–87.

[27] Van T. Lac and Katherine Cumings Mansfield, "What Do Students Have to Do with Educational Leadership? Making a Case for Centering Student Voice," *Journal of Research on Leadership Education* 13, no. 1 (2018): 38–58.

[28] Mitra, "Student Voice in Secondary Schools."

[29] R. R. Buss, "Exploring the Development of Students' Identities as Educational Leaders and Educational Researchers in a Professional Practice Doctoral Program," *Studies in Higher Education* 47, no. 6 (2022): 1069–83.

[30] Jean Anyon, *Radical Possibilities: Public Policy, Urban Education, and a New Social Movement* (Routledge, 2014).

[31] Derrick Bell, *Silent Covenants: Brown v. Board of Education and the Unfulfilled Hopes for Racial Reform* (Oxford University Press, 2004); Jake Burdick, Jennifer A.

Of course, as this book is about educational leadership, it is natural to include the stories of school network leaders, principals, district leaders, and one or two former US secretaries of education. I also chose leaders explicitly tasked with creating educational systems, who champion for diverse and underrepresented students and whose stories are about enacting systems-level initiatives that culminate in positive change at the individual level. There are also academics and activists whose secondary teachings have been life changing and perspective shifting to me and countless others. Some I had the privilege to take a class from. Their stories are de-academicized and approachable.

The professionals in public schools are not characteristic of the young people. Most larger school districts in the country are majority-minority. In the largest public school district, New York City (where I also lived for ten years and worked briefly at the Department of Education), 40% of students are Hispanic/Latinx, 26% are Black, 16% are Asian or Pacific Islander, and only 15% are white. In the third-largest US school district, Miami-Dade (where I currently reside), 73% of students are Hispanic/Latinx, 19% are Black, 1% are Asian or Pacific Islander, and only 6% are white. But current school leadership and teacher demographics do not represent the demographics of the student populations they serve.[32] Nationally, roughly 80% of US teachers identify as white and 77% of them as women.[33] And as one goes up the career ladder, leadership becomes more white and more male.

We must expand our notion of who educational leaders are and what leadership is in the broadest sense. To more accurately reflect student demographics, I used purposeful sampling to recruit storytellers, resulting in a disproportionately higher number of women and people of color and people with more variable geographic representation, age, and disciplinary background or position than in the field

---

Sandlin, and Michael P. O'Malley, eds., *Problematizing Public Pedagogy* (Routledge, 2013).

[32] M. Hansen and D. Quintero, *School Leadership: An Untapped Opportunity to Draw Young People of Color into Teaching* (Brookings, 2018), https://www.brookings.edu/blog/brown-center-chalkboard/2018/11/26/school-leadership-an-untapped-opportunity-to-draw-young-people-of-color-into-teaching/.

[33] National Center for Education Statistics, "Characteristics of Public School Teachers," US Department of Education, Institute of Education Sciences, 2023, https://nces.ed.gov/programs/coe/indicator/clr.

today. Purposeful boundaries[34] bring sharper focus to understanding how seasoned, sector-adjacent educational leaders (who are not primarily school or district administrators) advance equity-oriented change despite systemic barriers.

Scholar Jal Mehta reminds us that education is not standardizable. Enacting sustainable change and improving the conditions for all students to learn requires proximity to the problems and the desire to move beyond top-down reforms and toward shared accountability and empowerment.[35] That is my reason for including a wide variety of vantage points in education, each at a different level but each context- and problem-proximate. The stories these key stakeholders in education relate make complex ideas accessible, allowing me to bridge research, theories, and practice for you here. If you seek to remedy inequity, one of the narratives or part of a narrative in these chapters will help you find a solution. I hope the stories appeal to you and to all the aspiring educational leaders who pick up this book and that you find themes, strengths, and perspectives that resonate with and amplify your own.

Why Stories Matter

Stories like Denise's too often go untold, but they can spark meaningful change. Stories provide us with life lessons, and the narratives here distill key components of leadership and provide insight and optimism for those who aim to expand their capacities as leaders in education.

Many educators and school leaders describe teaching and leading as a bumpy road. They often look to colleagues with more experience to pick up lessons and tips scattered along the way. Recent research corroborates that having strong and close mentorship and learning from peers predicts teachers' future success.[36] This is one of the reasons

---

[34] Michael V. Singh, "Resisting the Neoliberal Role Model: Latino Male Mentors' Perspectives on the Intersectional Politics of Role Modeling," *American Educational Research Journal* 58, no. 2 (2021): 283–314.

[35] Jal Mehta, "From Bureaucracy to Profession: Remaking the Educational Sector for the Twenty-First Century," *Harvard Educational Review* 83, no. 3 (2013): 463–88.

[36] Matthew Ronfeldt, Katharine K. Matsko, Heather Greene Nolan, and Michelle Reininger, "Three Different Measures of Graduates' Instructional Readiness and the

I share stories; they are as close as some of us can get to working directly with a seasoned veteran. Stories, especially when from people we admire, allow us to sharpen our focus which sharpens our locus of control. Stories influence our—and stakeholders' and policymakers'—decisions because they make issues real and approachable.[37] The imagery in these stories will ideally serve readers to get as close as possible to wearing the leaders' shoes so they may recall these lessons when they need them the most. There's a stickiness to stories that makes them useful for solving real world problems.

In my journey to better understand educational leadership, I stumbled across what seems to be a slight but important void in the existing resources and literature used to educate and encourage leaders: plainly, there was a shortage of *stories*, of real tales told by people in the trenches who serve all students and the challenges they face. (Maybe part of this interpretation is rooted in a bias; I believe you can never have enough stories to pull from.)

Without real-world examples and knowledge to refer to, educational leaders might struggle to develop endurance to push beyond anxieties and adversities. Stories affirm that this work is intrinsically rewarding and purpose-driven, supporting hearts and minds in persisting within this ever-changing and challenging landscape.

Stories can offer us hope and hope is omnipotent.

During my doctoral training, my mentor, Dr. Pedro Noguera invited me to join him on a series of school visits across New York City, which he organized for a group of Alabaman educators. These were motivated, high-energy teachers and school leaders who admitted that it was incredibly tough for them to reach and connect with the youth of color from low-income backgrounds in the district they served. To expand the notion of what was possible, Pedro took us to a handful of Title I high schools (where most or even all students qualified for free or

---

Features of Preservice Preparation That Predict Them," *Journal of Teacher Education* 72, no. 1 (2020): 56–71; Matthew Ronfeldt, Sara L. Brockman, and Susanna L. Campbell, "Does Cooperating Teachers' Instructional Effectiveness Improve Preservice Teachers' Future Performance?," *Educational Researcher* 47, no. 7 (2018): 405–18.

[37] Silvia Gherardi, *How to Conduct a Practice-Based Study: Problems and Methods* (Edward Elgar, 2019); Anindya Kundu, "Fighting the Normalization of Failure," *Educational Leadership* 75, no. 6 (2018): 34–38.

reduced-priced meals). These schools served the poorest children in the city but sent nearly all of them to higher education by creating a culture that supported them and their various needs and uplifted their unique forms of giftedness. The schools thought of student well-being at every step and made structural changes that aligned with cultural needs.

For example, the schools extended the hours they were open, allowing families who needed flexible schedules to pick up their children on their time. Student work adorned the halls, and standardized tests were often waived for students who created portfolios of work that demonstrated their knowledge. Community professionals came to the school to offer workshops to students on printmaking, digital media production, culturally expansive culinary arts, and more. After seeing what could be done, the educators returned to Alabama excited to try new approaches, but most importantly, they were reminded that all kids are capable. The adage "seeing is believing" is full of truth.

The stories those Alabaman educators took back with them to their home state demystified leadership in practice. Examples in textbooks can feel distant, contextless, or too simplified for professionals to apply to their own contexts. While a chapter on email correspondences and communication power dynamics is certainly useful, these textbooks don't portray the range of duties and responsibilities bequeathed to educational leaders. Furthermore, these contexts change along with political, technological, and cultural developments.

This book gives you a chance to directly learn from others, like Denise, who you may not get the chance to meet and speak to in person. Although educational leadership as a field has brought forth many exciting and empowering concepts, strategies, and considerations for improving school and student outcomes, the modern educational ecosystem presents unique challenges for all stakeholders in education. Individuals in leading roles in classrooms, schools, and districts grapple with new political, social, behavioral, and health-related challenges.

The narratives presented in this book help us understand leaders' processes and motivations by providing a window to place, time, and space. In education, stories are particularly important because characters drive the plot and the process of learning. By telling here the stories of the leaders I interviewed, I share with you events as close to how they were experienced so you can get a feel for their contexts. I have written these in story form to reflect that we live storied lives.

Ideally, these stories will also produce contagious, feel-good effects reminding us that when people bind together, change is possible in the most difficult of circumstances. That is by design. Some may argue that research, objective and impartial, is not meant to produce such effects and I do not offer a retort. I simply want to note that sharing through storytelling is the most elementary and original way for us humans to grow and learn.

Stories help us address both routine and new challenges by showing us alternate ways things can be done. They provide parameters and definitions for the realm of possibility. As bell hooks once said, such "definitions are vital starting points for the imagination. What we cannot imagine cannot come into being. A good definition marks our starting point and lets us know where we want to end up."[38] Stories of success allow us to find the margins of possibility and workarounds to problems. If any of the stories make my readers say "So that's what it looks like!" or "I could do something similar!," the efforts of this book will have been worthwhile.

I hope that at least some of these vignettes will resonate with you, offering scenarios to apply to whatever you face. I have selected these stories specifically because they speak to common challenges and yet demonstrate extraordinary resilience and success. I am confident there is something for every reader in the forthcoming chapters.

Achievement and Well-Being for All

There's no argument about the importance of achievement for all students. Every single educator I've ever encountered wants each student to do well, and in the field of educational leadership, consensus grows for the primary goal being achievement for all students.[39]

---

[38] hooks, b, *Yearning: Race, gender, and cultural politics* (South End Press, 1990), p. 14.
[39] Colleen A. Capper and Elise M. Frattura, *Meeting the Needs of Students of ALL Abilities: How Leaders Go Beyond Inclusion*, 2nd ed. (Corwin, 2008); Terrance L. Green, "Community-Based Equity Audits: A Practical Approach for Educational

I now slightly expand the goal of promoting achievement for all to promoting achievement and well-being for all, an idea that I became more convinced of through my conversation with Jeffrey Duncan-Andrade (see Chapter 6). Well-being sustains achievement and success for people of all ages. Students rely on well-being to help them through the major life transitions they experience throughout their educational journeys, and educators require well-being to deal with the political, bureaucratic, and challenging organizational environments they operate within. It does educators no service to sugarcoat what they're up against in today's public schools, such as the war against "woke" and the nonacademic challenges students bring to the classroom with them.

Educators encounter systemic roadblocks, like a lack of school funding or overcrowded classrooms, that limit the amount of time, attention, and effort they can give to students. This can lead to feeling beaten down by the system and unconscious deficit thinking, believing that some students are less capable or worthy of learning than others, that students don't care about their future or self-improvement, or that teaching in communities with fewer resources is fighting a losing battle. Despair can take over our minds and bodies.

To overcome both the blatant and the nuanced personal, institutional, cultural, and structural barriers to equity and justice in the educational environment, we must exactingly and precisely inventory them. In *Viral Justice*, the sociologist Ruha Benjamin calls this necessary contending with reality *witnessing*: "In every case, before we can really appreciate the stubborn audacity and courage [improving a circumstance] takes, we have to look squarely, soberly, at what we're up against. I warn you, it ain't pretty... [Witnessing is] the surge of sorrow, rage, and weariness that comes each time we learn anew of the never-ending cruelties that surround us, that is our hearts breaking, each piece of our insides offering up a new surface—fresh understanding, greater

---

Leaders to Support Equitable Community-School Improvements," *Educational Administration Quarterly* 53, no. 1 (2017): 3–39.

resolve—connecting to our outsides."[40] Educators bear witness to the challenges that face students more than most. This can take a mental and physical toll and is why we must keep our health and well-being in mind.

But our interpretation of that adversity and how we move forward determines how adversity affects us. If we get bogged down by what we witness and cannot control when working for equity-driven, transformative change in education, our well-being is affected. The antidote is reasonable hope.[41] Learning from stories of success, such as those that follow, allows us to find the margins of possibility and to compile vetted workarounds to problems. Furthermore, hope is a trait that can be passed on to students. When our students have hope, they have higher self-esteem and perform at greater levels.[42]

The presence of hope and optimism among educational leaders leads to positive school climates, increased trust amongst stakeholders, and higher academic achievement and institutional success.[43] As philosopher Paolo Freire puts it, similar to sun and shelter, hope is an ontological need for humans.[44] In learning what those facing different challenges have found possible, this book proffers tools and knowledge to educational leaders to aid their pursuit of educational equity.

---

[40] Ruha Benjamin, *Viral Justice: How We Grow the World We Want* (Princeton University Press, 2022), 15.

[41] Jeffrey R. Duncan-Andrade, "Note to Educators: Hope Required When Growing Roses in Concrete," *Harvard Educational Review* 79, no. 2 (2009): 181–94.

[42] S. C. Marques, S. J. Lopez, and J. L. Pais-Ribeiro, "'Building Hope for the Future': A Program to Foster Strengths in Middle-School Students," *Journal of Happiness Studies: An Interdisciplinary Forum on Subjective Well-Being* 12, no. 1 (2011): 139–52; Peter Leeson, Joseph Ciarrochi, and Patrick C. L. Heaven, "Cognitive Ability, Personality, and Academic Performance in Adolescence," *Personality and Individual Differences* 45, no. 7 (2008): 630–35.

[43] Leigh McGuigan, "Principal Leadership: Creating a Culture of Academic Optimism to Improve Achievement for All Students," *Leadership and Policy in Schools* 5, no. 3 (2006): 203–29; Earl Johnson, Marcus Sanfilippo, Matthew Ohlson, and Anne Swanson, "Bridging the Optimism Gap: How Bringing Hope and Happiness into Schools Leads to Positive Changes," *Kappa Delta Pi Record* 55, no. 4 (2019): 184–90.

[44] Henry A. Giroux, "Paulo Freire's Pedagogy of Hope Revisited in Turbulent Times," *Postcolonial Directions in Education* 10, no. 2 (2021): 280–304.

Individual Agency Is Helping and Being Helped by *Others*

What unleashes the boundless potential of all students? Agency. Agency allows us to think positively and break out of the mold of deficit thinking and negativity.

Agency is so important that I devoted an entire book to the subject. In *The Power of Student Agency*, I argue that understanding what each child needs requires recognizing and nurturing their agency, or "a person's capacity to leverage resources to navigate obstacles and create positive change in their life."[45] I profile students who overcame immensely challenging structural obstacles related to growing up in poverty—drastic homelessness, incarceration, broken families, substance abuse, various traumas, undocumented citizenship—and blazed trails to obtain academic and professional greatness and financial stability.

Those stories substantiated my claim that more, or even all, students can achieve great things if they are supported and provided specific social and cultural resources. Approaches as simple as noticing and encouraging a student's particular giftedness are critical to providing young people an education that respects and empowers them.

In *The Power of Student Agency* I told the story of "Rose," who became homeless in her senior year of high school. Rose routinely experienced physical abuse by her father. When she confronted her parents about it, they kicked her out of their house. Rose managed to graduate from high school while sleeping on different friends' couches and eventually enrolled in community college. Here she met "Dr. Linden," who became a mentor to Rose in the science lab, helping Rose to finally start to trust adults again.

After many months, Rose told Linden her story and the two formed a close relationship over science. Linden helped Rose believe she was capable of accomplishing her ultimate goal of becoming a doctor. Without that support, Rose said, she might not have applied to college at the age of twenty-two, setting out on the hopeful path to medical school.

Stories such as this remind us that it costs nothing to recognize students' lived experiences and celebrate their journeys but benefits

---

[45] Kundu, *The Power of Student Agency*, xvii.

them enormously, but it allows them to visualize all the different ways that success could manifest for them. Sometimes all it takes is an encouraging conversation.

I call Rose and my other participants "exceptional, but not exceptions." Calling them *exceptions*, I reason, is a cop-out. It absolves us from taking on the system and makes the existing rules seem justified when they are not. If they're exceptions, the status quo is okay, when it is not. Instead, the students I profiled and those like them are *exceptional*, which other children can also become when we acknowledge their specific backgrounds, challenges, and identities in order to propel them to reach their potential.

I conclude *The Power of Student Agency* by making the case that uplifting underrepresented and disenfranchised groups benefits all of society, and that prioritizing success for each child, especially those with disadvantages, is critical to establishing a more just, equitable, and cohesive society. Better-educated communities are better able to tackle social challenges like climate change, overincarceration, lack of social safety nets, and poor health outcomes, while also making scientific and economic advances.

Similarly, in this book, I make claims that are based on stories of exceptional leadership in and around educational spaces. I argue that visionary leadership comes in all shapes, sizes, and job titles and that it can move what was believed immovable. In chapter summaries I analyze the stories with an agency framework and highlight how the storytellers tapped into their agency and fostered others'. Again, even these stories are not *exceptions*. There is no scarce or secret element behind developing world-class leadership, and leadership is as diverse and idiosyncratic as any human endeavor. But there are key takeaways, and armed with the right motivations, perspectives and strategies, we can *all* become higher-caliber leaders.

I now add three words to my previous definition of agency: it is "a person's capacity to leverage resources to navigate obstacles and create positive change in their life" and in others'.[46] And for a less academic definition, agency is a person's ability to create positive

---

[46] Kundu, *The Power of Student Agency*, xvii.

changes for themselves and others. The word "others" adds an incredibly necessary dimension to the equation of successful agency: social-level inputs that reach beyond an individual's life improvement and positively affect others. Even the strongest individual aptitude requires the right combination of additional supports to fully thrive.

Fostering another person's agency helps them find the relevance and excitement in their endeavors and then improve their circumstances. Leaders who have developed their agency have the ability to confront new challenges (explored in Chapter 5). They have learned from previous experiences and improved their capacities to lead others and their communities. In providing tools for addressing challenges leaders may encounter, I hope this book fosters your agency a little too.

Who Am I Accountable To?

Dr. Michelle Fine is one of the leading social psychologists in the US and a storyteller in Chapter 6. She told me during our conversation to ask, "Who am I accountable to?" before planning a direct course of action. The answer must consider one's professional, personal, and communal accountability, which roots us and focuses us on what and who matters. Keep in mind that it is an act of true bravery that parents and guardians willingly hand over their precious children to an institution with the hopeful assumption that they will be cared for—a gem offered to me in my conversation with Dr. Jeff Duncan-Andrade, whose story is featured in Chapter 6.

I have found that beginning my leadership classes with this question has been a fruitful and grounding exercise. As you make your way through this book, I encourage you to hold who you are accountable to in your mind in order to make the content more relevant to you.

I aim to make education more heartening. (I had to check that "heartening" is in fact a word because "disheartening" is more common; a symptom, no doubt, of the problem I am working to resolve.) My work addresses how people can overcome challenging situations at both the systems level and the interpersonal level, in formal group settings and between people in their relationships.

I approach educational leadership from a perspective of optimism, knowing that those of us who have been called to education have a deep desire to improve conditions and outcomes for children in our schools, from Pre-K through college. Young people are the primary reason most of us are drawn to education work; kids epitomize potential and personal growth. Children are often inherently less hardened by the realities of the real world. We see ourselves in their humanity and their willingness to learn from us. Whereas unequal outcomes for adults may not strike us with hot passion, children not given equal opportunity can rile us up and move us to demand change. I believe the field benefits from acknowledging our deeply rooted, structural limitations; to address and remove intergenerational inequities and barriers, we must think critically about which parts of the system only perpetuate the status quo. Today, prioritizing *justice*—an ever-moving target—necessitates having social and cultural competency in an incredibly diverse world and positioning all young people as inherently full of assets, not deficits.

At the heart of this book is the belief that, in times of tribulation, on a local, national, or global level, the human condition is still characterized by resilient service, routinely jumping over hurdles to smooth the path for those who follow. We can use the efforts of trailblazers before us as learning opportunities to strategize how to address problems of the current moment. Natural disasters, insufficient school resources, unexpected personal challenges, unmotivated staff members, or other, more invisible structural factors have challenged others when doing important work.

In education, the resilience of communities follows that of their leader. Strong leaders deeply understand their constituents' needs and their communities' potential. In these environments, more children feel as if they belong and act and flourish accordingly.[47] *This* is why these topics should matter to more of us; from *these* schools and *these* leaders spring a more whole and hale society.

A central argument in this book is that leadership and an individual's actions do not occur in a vacuum. Understanding leadership requires

---

[47] Reginald Green, *Practicing the Art of Leadership: A Problem-Based Approach to Implementing the Professional Standards for Educational Leaders* (Pearson, 2017).

understanding the social structures that encompass the actions. I pay close attention to the structural obstacles to my participants' goals, sharing with you how they worked around these obstacles. The takeaways and findings I present illustrate how leaders and aspiring leaders can access cultural and social tools that enable them to confront and work within the system, as well as leverage certain resources to change inequitable structures and accomplish their goals. This sociological lens is a relatively unique contribution in the field of educational leadership.

The positivity approach I'm laying out should feel natural to most readers of this book. Rightfully, we believe in schools and see them as a means to advance as a society because they are the main institution that develops children into future citizens. This belief instills in us an impulse for constant, iterative reform and school improvement.

These investments are of critical importance; the children of today will soon be the adults of tomorrow assuming the responsibility to create a better future for us all.

A Charge to My Reader

Did you pick up this book to increase your capacity as a leader? Or are you reading it to think about how to champion students or other underrepresented groups in innovative ways? Or maybe you're simply interested in compelling stories from some of your favorite scholars and advocates that you admire with hopes of being inspired. Whatever your motivations are, it stands to reason that eventually it will become necessary for you to draw on community to achieve your mission. Each story here involves the idea that integral social elements are behind leadership and that to be a leader you must recognize and recruit allies and be within existing coalitions or create them. We are social creatures, and education is perhaps our greatest collective social investment. Leadership cannot function in isolation, without a community to support it. Community shapes a leader's identity and purpose, especially during times of crisis and when adversaries are strong.

I invite you now to take a second to pause and reflect on the kind of leader you aspire to be (in any context) and the impacts you would like your work to have. More specifically, what traits do you intend to cultivate in *others*? Think about what kind of influence *you* would like to have on *your* stakeholders. What support do they need from you to be their best selves? What adjectives describe what you want to foster in your students, your colleagues, community members, complete strangers, or even naysayers? Do you want your stakeholders to become more "engaged," "determined," "prepared," "analytical," "curious," or "inspired"? What characteristics matter to *you*? Now hold that thought for a minute.

Even if you don't consider yourself a leader—yet—certain leadership traits are relevant to all aspects of life and any human pursuit. When you described the characteristics you hope to cultivate in your constituents, did you think about what it would take for you to embody those traits as well? If not, why not? That kind of self-reflection and self-awareness is critical for any leader to have.

How can you inspire others to develop these attitudes if you don't have them? A leader who embodies and models trust, authenticity, and humility empowers others through *servant* leadership.[48]

The same goes for education professionals across the gamut—how can an educational leader inspire creative or critical thinking without employing that kind of approach themselves? If we forgo professional development and fail to challenge ourselves to be truly committed to continual improvement, others will find it hard to be inspired by our leadership. To lead the way we must set the example and set the bar. As Aristotle said, "He who cannot be a great follower cannot be a great leader."

And so, first find what inspires you in order to unlock your potential to inspire others. You can't hold someone else accountable without first holding yourself to the same standards. For example, the onus is on me, the one presenting these lessons, to provide something worthy of your valuable time and attention, something that could fuel your fire so you too can kindle the flame in those you serve.

---

[48] Robert F. Russell, "The Role of Values in Servant Leadership," *Leadership and Organization Development Journal* 22, no. 2 (2001): 76–84; Dirk van Dierendonck, "Servant Leadership: A Review and Synthesis," *Journal of Management* 37, no. 4 (2011): 1228–61.

Bored leaders *bore* followers. Routines and mundanity hold us back, making us believe education is to be *endured* not *enjoyed*. Learning must be fun for it to become a lifelong endeavor. That's something we should want students everywhere to believe. But for them to believe it, we need to first believe it, too.

Overview of Chapters

The many and important theories in the field of the sociology of education inform our understanding of how people in real life can leverage resources to overcome interpersonal, institutional, and structural blockades and thus improve their chances to compete in the societal rat race. In Chapter 1, "The Sociology of Leading Systems Change," I discuss the value of educational leaders, obstacles they face, and how to overcome those obstacles. I present simple sociological frameworks that ground this book and bring the stories in following chapters to life in a more meaningful way for you. I relate the tale of a classroom library that dramatizes the debate over the influence of social structures versus human agency, the advantages of having social and cultural capital, and the merit in community and in collective efficacy.

One of my ongoing projects is a large qualitative exploration of educational leadership. As I seek to learn how to truly generate progressive change in education, I have met an endless number of inspiring individuals who truly walk the walk. I sifted through that material and selected special interviews that personify the themes of Chapters 2 through 6, the heart of the book, and wrote them into stories. I gathered from leaders—students, parents, school and district leaders, thought leaders, or prominent practitioners—these stories on how they identified impediments to success for all students and ameliorated them. Chapter titles indicate each of these themes and findings.

The storytellers in Chapter 2, "Build Better Systems," discovered the importance of meeting and prioritizing students' and stakeholders' basic needs above all else. Chapter 3, "Make Sense of the Nonsensical," covers the criticality of engaging in research processes, and how leaders identify problems, investigate solutions, and implement them. In Chapter 4, "Stick to Your Guns," storytellers defied the status quo to uphold their values and convictions, despite stressful pushback. Chapter 5, "Hand-Ups Over Handouts," contains stories of how leaders help students gain lifelong agency. The storytellers in Chapter 6, "Center Human Dignity," round out our themes, by showing how they champion the importance of a unifying value: that we uphold every person's dignity through advocating for them and their education. *Studying education* is a unique thing; it's quite meta, if you think about it. The goal is to *get educated* on *how people get educated*—to learn about *learning*. Organized learning separates our species from others in the animal kingdom; further, humans are able to *think* about what we are learning and doing, ideally to reflect and react accordingly. To echo Descartes, we think, therefore we *are*.

In the same vein, learning about how to become a better educational leader should allow you to pause, reflect, and subsequently sharpen your existing skill set and improve your environment. I structured this book with this goal in mind; at the end of each of the thematic chapters are summaries that encourage you to reflect on and go beyond the facts of each vignette. In the conclusion, Chapter 7, I share what I believe to be the stakes of this work, hopefully reminding you further why you and your leadership are so needed. At the end of this book is a toolkit to help you (and your students or other stakeholders) engage in deeper personal reflection to increase your leadership capacities—to take what you've learned from this book and apply it.

My highest aspiration for this book is that leaders turn to it on their journeys, whether daily errand or lifetime purpose, and find inspiration, reassurance, or brief moments of levity when things get tough. The leaders can be educational leaders or any other invested individual who cares to take a close look at how to navigate obstacles in the educational ecosystem today.

I

The Sociology of Leading Systems Change

Educational Leaders Maintain Our Social Fabric

Let's begin by defining foundational concepts that will bolster and contextualize the leaders' stories in subsequent chapters.

Education is any process through which learning takes place.[1] Ideally, a person is educated in a vibrant manner that inspires a desire for lifelong learning and motivation for continual self-improvement. One of the premises that this book rests on is that self-improvement itself is a systemic issue; everyone has a right to self-improvement, and as a society we are obligated to provide better institutions and pathways that allow those with less privilege to access right.

Schools are the institutions through which learning takes place. In them, students learn hard skills and cultural norms in addition to core academic knowledge.[2] Schools also are a primary site for socialization and conditioning so that communities can develop social norms, adding a heft to schools' influence beyond simply affecting individuals' lives.

---

[1] Hans-Peter Blossfeld and Jutta von Maurice, *Education as a Lifelong Process* (Springer, 2011); J. S. Bruner, *The Process of Education* (Harvard University Press, 2009).

[2] Jeffrey S. Dill, "Durkheim and Dewey and the Challenge of Contemporary Moral Education," *Journal of Moral Education* 36, no. 2 (2007): 221–37; Susan Fuhrman and Marvin Lazerson, eds., *The Public Schools* (Oxford University Press, 2005).

This gives schools an inherent power over the students and individuals they serve. Schools make decisions or are governed by decisions made by entities such as school boards, which will affect children's and communities' lives forever. Educational leaders are, then, a sort of ambassador of human development and social mobility.

But schools are not the sole proprietors of knowledge acquisition; much (if not most) learning takes place outside their walls. A student's life beyond school walls—including the circumstances of their home life, their access to healthcare and nutrition, and the safety and condition of their neighborhood—matter immensely to how well a student can perform *in* school.[3] It is critical that educational leaders realize this and create conditions in their school that lead students and staff to feel empowered to advance themselves everywhere else.

Mark Twain is often credited for the poignant statement "I never let schooling get in the way of my education." Relatedly, the enduring work of the Brazilian Paulo Freire still has relevance. He urged educators to make schools places where students become aware or societal limitations and liberate themselves from those obstacles to create a freer society for all.[4] School is a mechanism and an environment where we spend, for better or worse, our formative years. But those most attuned to the true mission of a school recognize that a school alone does not an education yield. A school is either a laboratory for learning or a holding place for stagnation, depending on the design. A good educational leader can create or support an exciting ecosystem for learning and then get out of the way for kids to thrive within and beyond that space.

---

[3] G. J. Duncan and R. J. Murnane, "Rising Inequality in Family Incomes and Children's Educational Outcomes," *RSF: The Russell Sage Foundation Journal of the Social Sciences* 2, no. 2 (2016): 142–58; A. Wade Boykin and Pedro Noguera, *Creating the Opportunity to Learn: Moving from Research to Practice to Close the Achievement Gap* (ASCD, 2011); Norm Fruchter, Megan Hester, Christina Mokhtar, and Zach Shahn, *Is Demography Still Desinty? Neighborhood Demographics and Public High School Students' Readiness for College in New York City* (Annenberg Institute for School Reform, 2012).

[4] Paulo Freire, "Pedagogy of the Oppressed," in *Toward a Sociology of Education* (Routledge, 2020), 374–86.

Vibrant schools create vibrant communities through a symbiotic relationship. These relationships and dependencies can exist with or without our active construction. Inequitable schools maintain or even create unjust and inequitable communities. A school leader must ensure that their locus of control, the school, is poised to promote equity and handle challenges that block it. These leaders have the potential to make the school a hub for the community.

The formalized education that schools provide—the concrete set of facts learned and skills gained by students—typically reflect the current needs and values of a society.[5] Whether schools and curricula actually keep up with the times is another matter altogether. Still, this is how schooling becomes political in nature; the considerations around what to teach, who to teach, how to teach, when to teach, and even why to teach can rile people up because of the potential impact on the future citizenry. And because nearly all of us will spend a significant portion of our waking lives as children and young adults in school, everyone's an expert in education in their own right, or at the very least has a vested interest in what is happening in schools. All of us are familiar with schools, and therefore their mystique and impact are almost impersonal. Educators and educational leaders are not always viewed as the authorities or maestros that they are.

A clear example of "armchair" expertise is the controversy surrounding the teaching of Michelangelo's masterpiece, David, in the spring of 2023 in a Florida school. Despite the international acclaim and historical significance of this Renaissance artwork, a Florida principal faced backlash and termination after parents labeled the statue "pornographic" when it was included in a lesson for a sixth grade class.[6]

---

[5] M. W. Apple and N. R. King, "What Do Schools Teach?," *Curriculum inquiry* 6, no. 4 (1977): 341–58.

[6] Tom Ambrose, "Florida Principal Who Quit Over David Statue Visits Florence to See 'Magnificent' Work," *The Guardian*, April 30, 2023, https://www.theguardian.com/us-news/2023/apr/30/florida-principal-david-statue-visits-florence.

This incident highlights how educators and educational leaders, in this case, the principal, may not always be recognized as the true authorities they are. Few of us claim to understand how to do a doctor's job, even though we've interacted with many doctors throughout our lives. However, the same professional respect is not similarly conferred on teachers. Armchair expertise informalizes and delegitimizes our perceptions of how much work it takes to get teaching right. As I write this from Florida in 2023, the state of Florida's education administration and governor have addressed our ongoing and massive teacher shortage through policies that lower the barrier to entry for teaching. One policy fills vacant positions with retired EMTs, veterans, and police officers, even without former teaching experience. Applicants must have attended *some* college but need to have maintained only a 2.5 G.P.A.[7] While these individuals would surely want to serve their students, they completely lack the rigorous training required to serve students well. It's one thing for a retired veteran to "manage" a classroom for a day or a week. It's a whole other thing to masterfully teach an eighth grade math class for an entire school year.

Many educators have personally told me that parents and others have given them advice on how to better do their jobs.

The reality of such power imbalances, and influence shifting away from education professionals, complicates educational leaders' heavy charge. Viewing educators as less than the professionals they are hinders them in preparing students for tackling the challenges of the future.

Educators' work affects communities universally, and what goes on in the classroom influences the attitudes, dispositions, and values of the upcoming generation. Everyone understands this. Some fear it. It makes sense, then, as US demographics rapidly change, that some resist broadening the scope of what it means to be an *American*, or at least one deserving of opportunity. The US from its inception has relied on immigration, but historically, only certain white immigrants have received a welcome, and the richness of others' ethnic stories has been discounted by various amounts at various times.

---

[7] Florida Department of Education, "Pathways to a Florida Educator Certificate," https://www.fldoe.org/teaching/certification/pathways-routes/ (accessed January 8, 2025).

Open discourse about what should and should not be taught in our public schools is a natural and healthy part of a democratic education. However, some voices have come to dominate education design. The contemporary knowledge bans that resulted represent a historical editing, one that, given schools' influence, could promote groupthink at best and fascism at worst.[8] We cannot hand our students rose-tinted glasses if they are to interrogate the world around them and develop into active citizens.

Take, for example, the long running battles on whether an ethnic studies curriculum is appropriate in public schools. Tucson's Mexican American Studies program highlighted the historical contributions of Hispanic citizens to the local community and raised the low achievement rates of students who participated.[9] In 2010, Arizona's governor, Jan Brewer, signed a law that banned the program. Fortunately, this ban was later ruled as an unconstitutional suppression of student rights by a federal judge.

Selective censorship is a threat to expanding students' worldviews. The American Library Association reported that 330 books were challenged in the fall of 2021 alone.[10] The majority of US book bans, as of 2024, stem from a handful of people. In Clay County, Florida, 100 book bans were instituted following complaints by a single person, and in one Utah school district, 199 of the 205 book bans were initiated by a single married couple, costing the district more than six figures in administrative efforts.[11] These people have no problem admitting that they do not read the books they take issue with.

---

[8] Willliam Black and Ira Bogotch, "Illiberal Democracy Has Now Come to Florida: What Can Academics Do?," *Journal of Educational Administration and History* 56, no. 4 (2024): 411–18.

[9] H. Stephenson, "What Arizona's 2010 Ban on Ethnic Studies Could Mean for the Fight Over Critical Race Theory," *Politico*, July 11, 2021, https://www.politico.com/news/magazine/2021/07/11/tucson-unified-school-districts-mexican-american-studies-program-498926.

[10] Z. Beauchamp, "Why Book Banning Is Back," *Vox*, February 10, 2022, https://www.vox.com/policy-and-politics/22914767/book-banning-crt-school-boards-republicans.

[11] "Hundreds of Books Are Usually Banned by Just ONE Person in a Community," Take Action for Libraries, April 20, 2023, https://action.everylibrary.org/books_are_often_banned_by_just_one_person_in_a_community.

Similarly, there has been a resurgence of debate around critical race theory (CRT) and even teaching basic racial history. In some states, again like Florida, the education departments have vetoed the teaching of AP African American history. These debates are thought to be a fear-mongering strategy from right-wing conservatives who claim students are being forced to learn age-inappropriate, complex legal frameworks like CRT.[12]

If we agree, as a majority does, that access to a high-quality education is and should be a universal American right—or even the *cornerstone* American right—then it seems only fair that students have the right to curricula that is inclusive, reflective, and factually honest. This means acknowledging the systemic inequalities groups have been subjected to as well as the contributions of those groups despite these disadvantages. Such curricula would naturally include uncomfortable realities. But those uncomfortable realities are part of the truth. It is okay for children to sit with such discomfort in order to grow. An education of any other kind would be called indoctrination.

A critical and balanced history of our nation's ongoing reckoning with race in the K-12 curriculum is necessary to adequately prepare students to learn from the wrongs of the past and present and strive to increase future opportunity for their fellow classmates. If we deny students truthful history and information, fearing it will make them feel uncomfortable, we are setting them up to act inappropriately when they have one-on-one encounters with people and ideas they are less familiar with.

In fact, without bringing students into this reckoning through age-appropriate yet critical curriculum on racial history, how can we ever hope to change the deeply baked systemic racism that still exists today—the likes of which folks like Denise Williamson confront routinely? The first step toward solving a problem is to admit and accept there is a problem. Our schools are where our future is being developed, and thus acknowledging and responding to our racial history is necessary to help all students achieve.

---

[12] J. C. Wong, "The Fight to Whitewash US History: 'A Drop of Poison Is All You Need,'" *The Guardian*, May 25, 2021, https://www.theguardian.com/world/2021/may/25/critical-race-theory-us-history-1619-project.

Functionalist and Conflict Perspectives Inform Grounded Leadership

The study behind this book is more than just about the factors that institute good leadership in *schools*. It is also largely about *civic* leadership. Education on some level has always been about civics and about so much more than pedagogy and classroom activities; in educational institutions, individuals perform backbone functions to maintain a vibrant and cohesive society. Schools are primary sites of democratic functioning, institutions that directly reflect both social progress and change.[13] The functionalist and conflict perspectives can help us to understand how effective education leaders are more than agents of student success.

The functionalist perspective, one of the classic and fundamental perspectives in sociology, speaks to this notion. Those in this camp are concerned with understanding what keeps societies and communities *functioning*. Schools and educational spaces are seen as upholding the democratic processes of societies by directly shaping *ideology*. The formal definition of ideology is that it is a set of common beliefs that give shape to how a community is run, informing economic and political policy.[14] Informally, we may think of ideology as being so conditioned in us that it is also the reason that we face the door after getting into an elevator or why women tend to go to the restroom in groups more than men do.

Most of the time, we think of this as a positive influence. Schools, through routine practices like the pledge of allegiance at assemblies, foster national ideals and help develop long standing norms about what matters to us as a collective. For example, at the turn of the twentieth century, some schools were specifically formed to create the idealized citizenry, promoting hygiene (likely to combat

---

[13] Émile Durkheim, *Education and Sociology* (Free Press, 1956); Peter Namphande, *Schools as Sites for Cultivating Democratic Citizens: Communication Through Learner Voice in Malawian Secondary Schools* (Routledge, 2021); John Gerring, "Ideology: A Definitional Analysis," *Political Research Quarterly* 50, no. 4 (1997): 957–94.

[14] Gerring, "Ideology."

the spread of disease), nationalism, and other cultural values at the time.[15]

Educative spaces uphold our national values, albeit in a nonlinear fashion, to different extents at different times. If national values and ideologies regress in antidemocratic directions—as it can be relatively easily argued is the case today—so does education policy.[16] The 1969 case *Tinker vs. Des Moines Independent Community School District* codified that teachers and students do not "shed their constitutional rights to freedom of speech or expression at the schoolhouse gate." Within reason—which is the key part up for recent debate it seems—individuals retain their right to free speech in schools as they do outside of them.

And of course, outside of informal practices and through the formalized curriculum, schools also stake a claim about what kinds of knowledge will matter as children transition into working, productive adults. This is one of the reasons I believe it's critical for schools to share these ideological responsibilities, specifically by forming partnerships and alliances with public and private sector organizations (healthcare agencies, companies who can offer students internships) to better, more holistically support students and ensure they're well rounded and ready to for the future. I'll elaborate on this idea when we finally allow ourselves to daydream about solutions in our conclusion.

Emile Durkheim is cited as the father of the functionalist perspective—and even if he is not the originator of the paradigm, he remains one of functionalism's main ancestors. Durkheim is known for regarding schools and other educational institutions (such as churches, even) as necessary to maintain social cohesion, integrate community members, and to foster a sense of satisfaction and belonging among those community members.[17] As an ambassador of these duties, a good

---

[15] Jennifer A. Rippner, *The American Education Policy Landscape* (Routledge, 2016).

[16] Jack Schneider and Jennifer Berkshire, *A Wolf at the Schoolhouse Door: The Dismantling of Public Education and the Future of School* (The New Press, 2020).

[17] Durkheim, *Education and Sociology*; Whitney Pope, "Durkheim as a Functionalist," *Sociological Quarterly* 16, no. 3 (1975): 361–79; Anthony R. Welch, "The Functionalist Tradition and Comparative Education," *Comparative Education* 2, no. 1 (1985): 5–19.

educational leader is one who deeply and critically understands their position for maintaining social cohesion both in their organization as well as within the broader community they serve.

So how do we even define the characteristics of the organization educational leaders serve and are a part of? Within a sociological framework, organizations can be seen as contexts that influence individuals' attitudes and behaviors. Organizations are seen as collective actors within the larger social system and as functioning structural units whose subunits create systems of interrelated parts (management theory, organizational effectiveness, systems theory). Organizations are "social structures created by individuals to support the collaborative pursuit of specified goals."[18] From an organizational standpoint of schools as socializing institutions, educational leaders play a pivotal role in the social cohesiveness of the school as an organization.

Given their instructional services and inherent power, schools are also instruments of *control*. Durkheim did argue that school discipline played an important part in conditioning children to learn rules and conformity[19]—an idea that perhaps has been taken too far/too literally, exemplified by the rapid proliferation of the school-to-prison pipeline (STPP) for many students of color from low-income backgrounds. It can also be easily argued that the STPP remains more of a racist instrument of control than one primarily concerned with students following the rules. But rather than support Durkheim's notions of fostering *cohesion*, the STPP and other coercive elements of schools seem to better support Karl Marx's thesis around *conflict*.

What separated Marx from Durkheim, and maybe continues to position him as the more notorious founder of sociology, is this conflict perspective, in which in a capitalist society, class conflict and clashing is seen as inevitable. And according to Marx, it is the elites—not the have-nots—who control ideology. To Marx and the generations of conflict theorists that followed, the ability to dictate ideology or the social narrative is one of the most dangerous tools that those

---

[18] W. Richard Scott, and Gerald Davis, *Organizations and Organizing: Rational, Natural and Open Systems Perspectives* (Routledge, 2015), 23.

[19] Joan Goodman, "School Discipline in Moral Disarray," *Journal of Moral Education* 35, no. 2 (2006): 213–30.

in power have because it can mollify the underclasses into thinking an unjust status quo is acceptable and necessary, rather than injustice.[20]

As the early twentieth-century Italian philosopher Antonio Gramsci put it, ideology can operate at the level of common sense, which can keep us from questioning injustices because they feel natural and are expected.[21] This is what makes ideology powerful, but also dangerous.

In *The Power of Student Agency*, I spent a considerable amount of energy debunking the underdeveloped, oversimplified, persistent "ideology of meritocracy," or the belief that the best, brightest, most hardworking, and most talented are the ones who achieve great things and climb the ladder. I do not delve as deep in this book, but I do say that these ideas set a trap that makes us ignore very real opportunity gaps, or inequitable access and/or inheritance to resources and opportunities. Worse still, the trap makes us inherently lay the blame for opportunity gaps at the feet of those who are victims to them. Meritocracy allows us to conveniently ignore that poverty is a *social*, not an individual, problem.[22]

We may see the overt jitteriness of a student as a sign of attention deficit disorder or disinterest, rather than notice the child lives in a "food desert" and maybe had candy and soda for breakfast and therefore underperforms.[23] And when driving by the panhandler on the road, we may not pause to think that their substance dependency is a product of disinvestment in their community leading to a lack of quality goods and services.

Another way of thinking about this is that often, the negative and suboptimal outcomes and conditions we notice are *downstream* effects. They are resulting from more structural, indelible phenomena which

---

[20] Alvin W. Gouldner, *The Dialectic of Ideology and Technology: The Origins, Grammar, and Future of Ideology* (Oxford University Press, 1982).

[21] Kate Crehan, *Gramsci's Common Sense: Inequality and Its Narratives* (Duke University Press, 2016).

[22] Matthew Desmond and Bruce Western, "Poverty in America: New Directions and Debates," *Annual Review of Sociology* 44, no. 1 (2018): 305–18.

[23] Seth E. Frndak, "An Ecological Study of Food Desert Prevalence and 4th Grade Academic Achievement in New York State School Districts," *Journal of Public Health Research* 3, no. 3 (2014): 319.

occur *upstream*.²⁴ This is a relatively new idea in social sciences largely stemming from public health. When a patient comes to a healthcare facility showing signs of lead poisoning, it does not necessarily mean they chose to ingest lead. More likely, they inhabit spaces (schools, apartments) that have lead-based contaminants such as paint. Distressed and deformed fish in a lake perhaps indicates a power plant polluting the water upstream.

Equally, it is a dangerous assumption to believe that those at the top are only there because of inherent skills and excellence, and not as a reflection of privilege and gatekeeping across racial, gender, language, class, and other divides. Billionaires Elon Musk, Jeff Bezos, and Kim Kardashian each had some financial support from their parents that helped them in the earliest stages of their careers. Meritocracy leads to the willing creation of gaps between those with privilege and those without. This train of thought also inequitably applies the same rules or assumptions about how success or wealth should be achieved, with motivation the compelling reason for achievement/underachievement, while ignoring barriers and biases that so many groups have historically dealt with and still do today.

This is why it is important to challenge the notion that achievement is only an individual pursuit, rather than collective. Thinking of some students as exceptions instead of exceptional subtly implies they may not need our help when in fact all students need support. It makes the rules in place seem justified. I am writing this book as part of my endeavor to fight against some of these unjust rules that govern us.

Opportunity gaps are "shortages in life opportunities—related to accessing quality education of course, but also health, occupational, and relationship outcomes—which result from differences people inherit with respect to their race, ethnicity, gender, and socioeconomic status."²⁵ To personify opportunity gaps, in 2014, Dr. Pedro Noguera and I wrote an opinion editorial titled "Why Students Need More Than

---

²⁴ Naoimh E. McMahon, "Framing Action to Reduce Health Inequalities: What Is Argued for Through Use of the 'Upstream–Downstream' Metaphor?," *Journal of Public Health* 44, no. 3 (2022): 671–78.

²⁵ M. Akiba, G. K. LeTendre, and J. P. Scribner, "Teacher Quality, Opportunity Gap, and National Achievement in 46 Countries," *Educational Researcher* 36, no. 7 (2007): 369–87Click here to enter text.; R. N. Johnson-Ahorlu, "The Academic

Grit" for MSNBC.[26] This was during the height of the "grit craze." We used the example of Miguel Fernandez, a student at the top of his class, loved by all teachers, who had to work at McDonald's instead of going to college because of his undocumented status. Miguel had been a US resident for most of his life, but alas, did not have the papers to prove that the United States was *his* country. His circumstances were unrelated to merit, yet they enforced reduced opportunities for him.

Marxian sociologists of education contend that schooling systems in a capitalist society only serve to reproduce inequality. Studies have shown that parental level of education predicts a child's educational and economic attainment more than parental income or the child's IQ.[27]

Social reproduction theory argues that schools maintain the existing social order and *perpetuate* inequality in a capitalist framework such as ours, where school funding is based on tax lines.[28] The United States lags many developed nations on the Program for International Student Assessment (PISA) test, but if poverty rates were controlled, students' scores could catch up to the rest of the world across subject matters.[29] Schools alone cannot solve *social* issues.

In the American historical context, class and race are intertwined, as there has always been a disproportionate distribution of resources. Of course, the US does not even become a world superpower if not for

---

Opportunity Gap: How Racism and Stereotypes Disrupt the Education of African American Undergraduates," *Race Ethnicity and Education* 15, no. 5 (2012): 633–52

[26] Anindya Kundu and Pedro Noguera, "Why Students Need More Than Grit," MSNBC, https://www.msnbc.com/msnbc/my-brothers-keeper-education-msna276431.

[27] Samuel Bowles and Herbert Gintis, *Democracy and Capitalism: Property, Community, and the Contradictions of Modern Social Thought* (Basic Books, 1986); Samuel Bowles and Herbert Gintis, "The Inheritance of Inequality," *Journal of Economic Perspectives* 16, no. 3 (2002): 3–30.

[28] P. Bourdieu, "Cultural Reproduction and Social Reproduction," in *Knowledge, Education, and Cultural Change: Papers in the Sociology of Education*, ed. Richard Brown (Routledge, 2018); E. J. Dixon-Román, *Inheriting Possibility: Social Reproduction and Quantification in Education* (University of Minnesota Press, 2017).

[29] H. L. Fleischman, P. J. Hopstock, M. P. Pelczar, and B. E. Shelley, *Highlights from PISA 2009: Performance of US 15-Year-Old Students in Reading, Mathematics, and Science Literacy in an International Context* (National Center for Education Statistics, 2010).

slavery, where abundant resources were created and not distributed at all to those producing them. But there has also been the more subtle and immensely impactful subsequent legislation, such as the G.I Bill where white veterans were supported to purchase middle-class homes that lead to generational property ownership and wealth, and Black veterans were not.

Thus here, where race has always been used as a means to separate, social reproduction within schools also explains much of the persistent racial achievement gap. "Rebellious" and justice-oriented frameworks like CRT, as well as the collective actions they help to mobilize, can help us recognize these pathologies and feel compelled to do something about them. To me, this is also undoubtedly why these schools of thought are seeing the pushback I mentioned earlier by dominant groups who feel threatened (even including white moderates and liberals) by CRT and the like.[30]

There is a pattern of frameworks being attacked before for being dangerous. In 2019, there was a fight against intersectionality studies and approaches which were (unfoundedly) positioned as an explicit attack on white men.[31] In reality however, intersectionality studies recognize that an individual can hold multiple identities simultaneously (i.e., race, gender, ableness) and experience compounded marginalization from how those identities intersect.[32] Sumi Cho, Kimberlé Crenshaw, and Leslie McCall argue that the goal of intersectionality is to "[expose] how single-axis thinking undermines legal thinking, disciplinary knowledge production, and struggles for social justice," through convenient exclusion—both de jure (by law) and de facto (by practice).[33] Relatedly, our inability to transcend single-axis thinking maintains structural inequality and glosses over the multidimensional nature of

---

[30] A. Seitz-Wald, "In Virginia, Republicans See Education Curriculum Fears as a Path to Victory," NBC News, 2021, https://www.nbcnews.com/politics/elections/virginia-republicans-see-education-curriculum-fears-path-victory-n1281676.

[31] Jane Coaston, "The Intersectionality Wars," *Vox*, May 28, 2019, https://www.vox.com/the-highlight/2019/5/20/18542843/intersectionality-conservatism-law-race-gender-discrimination.

[32] Sumi Cho, Kimberlé Crenshaw, and Leslie McCall, "Toward a Field of Intersectionality Studies: Theory, Applications, and Praxis," *Signs* 38, no. 4 (2013): 785–810.

[33] Cho et al., "Toward a Field of Intersectionality Studies," 787.

American society, history, and experience that naturally arises from our proud claim to be a melting pot but which we do not reflect in our practices and policies.

Without the multidimensional-axis allyship of institutions and organizations that try to understand the multiple factors stacked against underprivileged students, schools are less able to create a just social order serving their diverse students equitably. For example, if a school could provide access to a free dental clinic nearby or on site, students with debilitating toothaches and without healthcare could still learn; those structural obstacles are a very real part of their reality. Dr. Angela Duckworth shares an experience illuminating a similar problem in Chapter 2. The same goes for mental health services, arts and sports programs, and any kind of services that our young people should be granted to lead happy and fulfilling lives.

To me, the one place where we as a *society* can afford to be a little more socially minded is in education where our children go to receive nurture and care. The leaders whose stories I share in the forthcoming pages generally believe that achievement and opportunity are mutually dependent and far from *not* mutually exclusive.

When I first started grappling with the idea that education and US schools were more likely to worsen and not break cycles of poverty, it hit me hard. My whole life I had been conditioned by the egalitarian ideology that through our public education system, the best and brightest can still come out on top, regardless of background. This concept was so ingrained in me that it felt commonsensical; after all, my achievements are what had brought me academic success. Or so I thought.

I knew poverty was an obstacle, but I didn't realize how much of a roadblock it could be, embedded deep under the structures that impact schooling and which schools poor students attend. In my childhood, I felt comfortable that my straight As and student body president accolade got me into the University of Chicago. I now realize that my admission to better schools as my dad got promotions and took us into a wealthier neighborhood was monumental in terms of my access to opportunities.

You see, if you've been appropriately rewarded for your efforts throughout your life, it might be harder to realize that the same doesn't apply to other people with different levels of privilege. It is not that those people are starting a few steps back in the sprint; some were not invited to participate and others' legs were shackled in cuffs. Why then is their failure to compete and complete so often seen as a failure of individual responsibility?

It wasn't until I started to notice the bleak conditions of the neighborhoods that surrounded our university and I became interested in crime and inequality research that the impact of these enduring struggles started to become clearer. In that 2020 TED Talk that inspired Denise Williamson to reach out to me, I mentioned that my first job out of college was as a researcher for a project that took place in the Cook County Juvenile Temporary Detention Center (JTDC) on the West Side of Chicago—the largest youth facility of its kind in the country. I helped process youth at the Intake Center and randomly assigned some to receive cognitive behavioral therapy (CBT).

The youth came from the same impoverished neighborhoods in Chicago and were 99% Black and Brown.[34] The recidivism rate was through the roof, with some of the kids coming back to the center for minor crimes and offenses more than a dozen times by the time they turned fifteen. I secretly wanted to assign all the students to the CBT program because chances were good that it might help them, and then why need to do a multi-year trial? In the end, the trial did prove to be a highly cost-effective intervention: CBT and associated measures were correlated with a 21% decrease in readmission/recidivism to the facility.

At the JTDC, I noticed that most of the kids, when comfortable, were bright, funny, and boisterous. Every day, I felt like I was conducting an ethnographic study from the other side of the glass that separated us—me in the intake processing room and the youth in a holding cell. Seemingly, what they lacked was *opportunity*. Born a few blocks away from better schools and nicer roads, these young people could have been students for longer if they had had the chance.

---

[34] Sara B. Heller, Anuj K. Shah, Jonathan Guryan, Jens Ludwig, Sendhil Mullainathan, and Harold A. Pollack, "Thinking, Fast and Slow? Some Field Experiments to Reduce Crime and Dropout in Chicago," *Quarterly Journal of Economics* 132, no. 1 (2017): 1–54.

Maybe some of them could have even been honors students. But then they fell into the slow churn of the (uncorrecting) correctional system.

And then a little more than a decade after my ideological revelations, Denise Williamson reminded me that sometimes even the best and brightest are not given the option to get ahead. They are intentionally tracked away from prestigious colleges and tracked toward unfavorable outcomes, even including juvenile detention. Our system can be more exclusionary than inclusionary.

Ideology and our mainstream notions directly affect perceptions of educational achievement and what students are capable of, which in turn affects our approaches and policies. This is why in my career I expose our unproductive infatuation with grit, resilience, and self-control. Basically, overemphasizing individualism as key to success puts the onus mostly on the student, blaming them if they fail, when we should instead create a warm embrace of support.

Grit comes after a child's basic needs are met—after they are clothed, fed, sheltered, and loved; until then, how can a student demonstrate adequate self-control, or even sit still in class, if they haven't had a nutritious meal before school? How can a student demonstrate the growth mindset needed to study for a math test if their caretaker had to work a night shift and so the student had to help younger siblings before they could study? What if these students are displaying grit and resilience of a different kind, one steeped in empathy, love, and hope—an atypical kind that we should recognize and nurture in our schools?

When we say that student A has resilience but student B does not, we're more likely to blame student B for perceived laziness, lack of concern for their future, or some other unfair personal failure. But they might simply need more support to develop and learn all of the behaviors that would unlock their true hidden potential. We do a disservice as educators when we believe that *achievement* is all about the individual student and their abilities; this makes us think the achievement gap is *their* problem. Instead, using the word "opportunity" allows us to take social contexts into account; calling it an opportunity gap allows us to work against our ingrained tendencies and our ideological conditioning to realize we can all do more in the name of educational equity.

To usher in socially progressive change and inclusive conditions for diversifying student populations, a growing wave of scholarship studies disruptive and transformative educational leadership (in particular, see the work of Carolyn Shields).[35] Disrupting and challenging the status quo appears to be gaining steam in leadership research,[36] and researchers tackle complexities from structural racism to student wellness. Rather than adopting the management style of transactional leadership, educational leaders should move toward transformational leadership that builds the capacity of each stakeholder rather than fostering dependency on singular leaders.[37]

I say all of this to acknowledge that being an educational leader is anything but easy. Educational leaders work in the trenches, devoting their energy to a system that has been set up in such a way that moves the primary focus away from supporting all students. They must stick with their ideals and lead with the courage and conviction that they know what's best for their stakeholders and the community they are a part of.

An educational leader has the lofty task of weaving key parts of our democratic fabric but also directly serving at the ground level. The work they do is both functionalist, to keep operations smooth, and conflict-oriented, to understand that schools may not always be egalitarian and can perpetuate inequality. The weight of these acknowledging these aspirations can propel educational leaders to break unjust cycles and create conditions for all students to thrive. These ideas should, above all, make it clear that the work of educational leaders does matter, in more ways than one, and that they truly are consummate professionals in our communities.

---

[35] Carolyn M. Shields, *Transformative Leadership in Education: Equitable and Socially Just Change in an Uncertain and Complex World* (Routledge, 2017).

[36] K. Neville and K. B. Taylor, "Disrupting the Status Quo: Developing an Equity-Oriented Educational Leadership PhD Program," *About Campus* 28, no. 6 (2024): 41–44.

[37] Carolyn M. Shields, *Transformative Leadership in Education: Equitable, Inclusive, and Quality Education in an Uncertain and Complex World* (Taylor & Francis, 2024).

The Structure-Agency Dichotomy Meets Debra's Kindergarten Classroom Library

In sociology, a classic disciplinary debate is whether social structures have or human agency has more influence in determining the outcomes within the rat race of human life. *How much can I actually control my future destiny?* Sociologists, including myself, are obsessed with structures. This is not to be confused with deficit ideology and thinking deterministically, but rather aligned to understanding that only through assessing our limits can we reach our possibilities.

Structures are all around us, made up of groups of institutions—the most basic forms of social structures include neighborhoods and how they are districted, the economy, our legal system, and even race. For some, structures could be *enabling*; for instance, if someone has more of a social safety net (often manifesting into direct forms of economic capital, such as a trust fund), they can take more risks and not work a job to make ends meet and not worry about how to afford college. But most of the time, structures are considered *limiting*.

A student's birth zip code and their caregivers' income are of the strongest predictors of that young person's future educational attainment and job prospects. Intergenerational inequality is often rigid and inflexible, and thus persistent.[38] If our educational systems were honestly fulfilling their egalitarian burden, this would not be the case because we would see greater social mobility across social class. But we don't; those at the bottom income quartiles are much more stagnant than those at the top.

Schools are *built into* the social structures and social fabric—they are less able to influence their surroundings (e.g., a low-income student's college options) than their surroundings influence them (e.g., a disinvested neighborhood is likelier to have schools with subpar

---

[38] G. J. Duncan and R. J. Murnane, "Rising Inequality in Family Incomes and Children's Educational Outcomes," *RSF: The Russell Sage Foundation Journal of the Social Sciences* 2, no. 2 (2016): 142–58; Fruchter et al., *Is Demography Still Destiny?*; R. Chetty and N. Hendren, "The Impacts of Neighborhoods on Intergenerational Mobility I: Childhood Exposure Effects," *Quarterly Journal of Economics* 133, no. 3 (2018): 1107–62.

building conditions, obsolete technology, and science equipment, underpaid and thus undermotivated staff, and scarce and tattered books for students).

A totally structuralist perspective, heady as that might sound, holds that this all matters because it means that educational leaders' influence is limited. Structuralists are pragmatists. But because of this, perhaps they are also *pessimists*. There is likely a better, more *hopeful* approach, especially when it comes to achieving progressive change when it seems like all the odds are stacked against it. As structures themselves are man-made, they can also perhaps be woman-taken-down!

Let me tell you quickly about one of my former students, Debra Bazile. Debra is an elementary school teacher and reading coach. When she first began her teaching career, she taught at an elementary school in Little River, Miami, a Title I school, which means it serves predominantly students of color from low-income homes. Debra quickly realized how much her new students loved storytime in class. She decided to institute a class library policy where students could check out books from the classroom, take them home, and then bring them back to exchange for another book.

After a little while, a problem emerged: the books were going home, but they were not coming back to school. Debra asked herself, "Why is this happening?" and though she could have found fault and deficiency in her students, who on face value were keeping things that did not belong to them, she instead looked for fault in the system and the structures that be.

Debra started with the most obvious fact, that these students loved to read but did not have any books at home. She saw this as an opportunity gap which she chose to fill through bringing more books into the scenario. She partnered with her school and local library to get more books donated to the class and to get her students library cards. Because Debra increased more books at the source, students did not fear that the books would run out. Eventually, all the books were coming back to class and the classroom library was vibrant, exceeding Debra's expectations (see Figure 1.1). Everyone was happy.

Through leveraging her own agency—using social and cultural resources to overcome a barrier—Debra increased her students' as well.

FIGURE 1.1 A few images from Debra's classroom during the 2024–2025 school year. Courtesy of Debra Bazile.

She found support in her community, engaging more hands to overcome a structural challenge. Her students, armed with library cards, not only learned how to borrow books properly, but they also learned how limitations can be overcome through the power of the collective.

Similarly, educational professionals are constantly confronted by various challenges—often more serious than books not returning to school—which derail their best laid plans and efforts. These obstacles can get in the way of leaders' abilities to enact change toward achievement for all. Educational leaders must remain steadfast in their goals often by maintaining a long focus on the horizon, brushing off and learning from the various inevitable and disheartening setbacks, and always being open to recognizing which partners, resources, or opportunities that are in their midst. I enjoy studying agency because it is rooted in hope triumphing over despair, which characterizes human endeavor.

An agency perspective is inherently positive and glass-half-full; it believes in the potential of individuals to positively impact their environment, rather than focusing on what competencies may be lacking. Agency can be used to counter rampant *deficit* perspectives in education—that some students, teachers, or some schools are unable to or unworthy of achieving.[39] Applying agency frameworks requires identifying structural obstacles, strategizing workarounds, and thus better articulating the realm of possibility.

Agency implies the existence of barriers (often structural) to transcend, and that is also what separates it from other forms of generalized action.[40] Generalized action in Debra's story would be to cancel the classroom library after reprimanding her students, only for similar challenges to arise again and for children's spirit to be crushed in the process. An agency approach, on the other hand, must be context specific.

As Pedro Noguera says, a "pragmatically optimistic" perspective acknowledges the possibilities for systemic improvement in education but also the necessity to first admit and recognize that structural

---

[39] Clifford Geertz, *The Interpretation of Cultures* (Basic Books, 1973); Anindya Kundu, *The Power of Student Agency: Looking Beyond Grit to Close the Opportunity Gap* (Teachers College Press, 2020).

[40] Geertz, *The Interpretation of Cultures*; William H. Sewell Jr., "A Theory of Structure: Duality, Agency, and Transformation," *American Journal of Sociology* 97, no. 1 (1992): 1–29.

obstacles exist." That intersection is where a pragmatically optimistic educational leader could thrive. But someone can only develop a flourishing classroom library when t5hey pause to consider why the books are not returning to school in the first place.[41]

Fostering Agency and Mobilizing Forms of Capital as a Guiding Theoretical Framework

The stories I collected for this book are part of my continued scholarly pursuit to operationalize the foundational concept of agency, which has been historically theoretical and difficult to identify in practice.[42] The agency of educational leaders is vital to the achievement of all students and their successful outcomes.

Innate psychology and external social factors shape each person's agency. Everyone has agency as early as birth that is based on factors like nature and nurture, the environment as well as experience.[43] We all have the ability to pursue what interests us; we only need a little direction to own the path.

As a new dad I get to see this playing out in front of my eyes. My daughter, Mika, started crawling first and encouraged my son, Jai, to join her—sometimes taunting him with a toy he wanted. As I write this, Mika is taking her first steps and Jai is still moving at his own pace, happy to be crawling. When we read to them Jai is more able to be still, and Mika's frenetic energy has her grabbing impatiently at the pages.

Throughout childhood, young people use their experiences to test out how to act, finally developing into adults capable of contributing meaningfully to the world. Prominent sociologist George Herbert

---

[41] Pedro A. Noguera, "Schools, Prisons, and Social Implications of Punishment: Rethinking Disciplinary Practices," *Classroom Management in a Diverse Society* 42, no. 4 (2003): 341–50.

[42] Steven Hitlin and Hye Won Kwon, "Agency Across the Life Course," in *Handbook of the Life Course*, ed. Jeylan T. Mortimer and Michael J. Shanahan (Springer, 2006); Sewell, "A Theory of Structure."

[43] Anindya Kundu, "Understanding College 'Burnout' from a Social Perspective: Reigniting the Agency of Low-Income Racial Minority Strivers Towards Achievement," *Urban Review* 51 (2019): 677–98; Kundu, *The Power of Student Agency*.

Mead postulated that though the human is innately self-centered and self-serving, interacting with others in the social world refines one's personality and dispositions.[44] Mead saw "self" as a process, which is a nice way of thinking about it because it leaves room for improvement.[45] This is also why *play* is so important—for kids *and* adults—so they can experiment with the boundaries of norms and expectations while having fun and figuring out *who* they are.

My research also indicates that tailored forms of social and cultural capital help students form productive goals that facilitate their achievement. Social and cultural capital are noneconomic resources—meaning that largely, they cannot be bought.[46] As such, these forms of capital are mostly related to *socialization*; the social world and our interactions with others give social and cultural capital inherent value and increase our ability to pursue and receive rewards, like acceptance (e.g., informally in friend groups or formally through a job offer).

In *The Power of Student Agency*, I summarized the basic ways of social and cultural capital:

> Social capital consists of relationships between group members, manifesting through shared understanding of social norms and pooled resources that are mutually beneficial. Social capital can also be thought of as access to different social networks and the benefits derived from participation in those networks (e.g., information and support). Cultural capital is defined as nonfinancial assets that promote a person's social mobility beyond economic means. Cultural capital can be thought of as using one's symbolic toolbox and knowing how to (consciously and subconsciously) use language and behavior in different, complex social settings . . . I often tell students to think of social capital as the connections that can get you into the annual Met Gala,

---

[44] George Herbert Mead, *Mind, Self, and Society from the Standpoint of a Social Behaviorist* (University of Chicago Press, 1934).

[45] Herbert Blumer, "Sociological Implications of the Thought of George Herbert Mead," *American Journal of Sociology* 71, no. 5 (1966): 535–44.

[46] Pierre Bourdieu, "Cultural reproduction and social reproduction," In *Education and the State: Volume 1: Schooling and the National Interest*, ed. Roger Dale, Geoff Esland, and Madeleine MacDonald (pp. 56–68) (Routledge & Kegan Paul, 1986).

whereas cultural capital is knowing how to conduct yourself when you are there.

Educational spaces can provide these forms of capital for free. The story of "J-Stud" describes this in real life.[47] J-Stud was a young man who grew up in a fatherless home in a low-income neighborhood of Jamaica, Queens. He got in trouble and fights throughout primary school and was slowly tracked into special education. Sitting in the back of all his classrooms, keeping his head down over a tattered notebook, he felt disconnected from school.

Enter J-Stud's tenth grade English teacher. She asked if she could see what he was scribbling so furiously in the notebook. Hesitantly, J-Stud showed her page upon page of rap lyrics. She saw talent and presented J-Stud with the opportunity to record music at her friend's studio if he put in basic effort in her class. J-Stud agreed and eventually performed for his classmates, who gave him a standing ovation. J-Stud's teacher, using her social capital (connections at the studio), opened doors for him. A teacher who prioritized rewarding certain, typical forms of social and cultural capital, ones reproducing the status quo would have overlooked J-Stud.

We must work to broaden what kids can visualize for themselves. Young men of color growing up in the Bronx walk by Yankee Stadium every day. If they dream of playing baseball in the Major Leagues, that reflects their lived realities and limited opportunities. In actuality, only 1 in 200 high school baseball players gets drafted by a professional team.[48]

At the same time, we must understand representation is a structural issue before we can address students' perceptions of themselves. The public school teaching force is drastically less diverse than the student population, and the higher status the position, the more white it becomes. Students see this and internalize it. If no Black males teach or

---

[47] Kundu, *The Power of Student Agency*.

[48] Mike Rosenbaum, "Examining the Percentage of MLB Draft Picks Who Reach the Major Leagues," *Bleacher Report*, June 13, 2012, https://bleacherreport.com/articles/1219356-examining-the-percentage-of-mlb-draft-picks-that-reach-the-major-leagues.

lead in their school, how does a Black male student come to think of themselves as capable of teaching?

What is perhaps most remarkable about J-Stud's story is what happened after high school. At the studio, J-Stud met a couple of folks who took him under their wing and showed him the ropes of the business. The young man found himself drawn to the accounting side of the business and he was invited to spend his summers working at the studio while he attended the local community college to get his associate's degree in accounting. Through his new mentors, he eventually met others in the finance world. Some of these helped J-Stud get a high-profile internship that would pay for his college degree in business and finance. Today, J-Stud is a managing director at one of the largest banks in New York City, but he still lives in Queens so that the neighborhood kids can see a different example of what they could one day be. J-Stud shows us that success does not have to mean leaving your community behind; it can lift them up as you begin to soar.

Although we would hope that each J-Stud will meet a life-changing English teacher, we cannot leave that to chance. Instead, we should create systems that make the development of these relationships more natural and seamless.

The same ideas apply to education leaders. Similar to students, all leaders start with a locus of agency and control over their circumstances. Their agency is tied to their identity and passion and motivation for being an educational leader and the long journey to get there. They have a more established idea of their goals but need resources to make their dreams a reality. In the vignettes that follow, I highlight for you how the storytellers tapped into social and cultural capital to unleash their agency and that of others. I share with you a simple framework to begin thinking about how we can expand our capacities toward this endeavor. I discuss free tools that can be leveraged to meet equity goals. Both novice and seasoned leaders will find them useful in re-realizing their goals.

Research that looks to identify the agency within people provides hope and inspiration for leaders to take the reins in challenging times, but with asset- and equity-based approaches at the center of their practice. Though there are countless, amazing resources for how to be an effective leader who promotes equity in education and the well-being of all students and staff,[49] I am not aware of any books on leadership in education that use qualitative, sociological, narrative research in the manner I do—bringing together different leaders across educational levels, locales, sectors, and professions—to share their inspiring stories while highlighting how these everyday people mobilized forms of capital to obtain their desired ends.

Collective Efficacy: A Pivotal Source of Support and Metric of Collaboration

Education leaders are at the forefront of dealing with structural-level and interpersonal conflicts in their schools. For example, they may contend with the mental and physical health effects of students having to live and walk through high-crime neighborhoods on their way to school or living in a food desert with limited access to nutritious food. At the same time, these leaders constantly manage the interpersonal and behavioral challenges of others, including negotiating workplace conflicts and disputes, hierarchical and chain-of-command issues, and communication problems among staff and/or students.

As the stories that follow will remind you, juggling all of this is especially hard when things get tough, tensions rise, and the group starts to fray. Because a leader's personality and approach influences that of others, a leader must not only manage others but also themselves to lead effectively.

Of course, then, the desire to suit up and lead students and staff every day is a conscious and brave choice. As a strong leader you are okay with criticism, go against the grain when it's not popular, and stand firm in

---

[49] Some include Shelly Burgess, *Lead Like a Pirate: Making School Amazing for Your Students and Staff* (Dave Burgess Consulting, 2017); Ken Williams, *Ruthless Equity: Disrupt the Status Quo and Ensure Learning for ALL Students* (Wish In One Hand Press, 2022); and Eric Jensen and Carole Snider, *Turnaround Schools for the Teenage Brain: Helping Underperforming Students Become Lifelong Learners* (Jossey-Bass, 2013).

your convictions in the name of student betterment. This also means you can and must be vulnerable.

Perhaps more than in other fields like politics, in *education*, leaders cannot simply be authoritative or charismatic to attract and command followers; though those are certainly approaches to leadership, they cannot be all of leadership.[50] The pursuit of creating a culture that prioritizes student success, and the success of students from diverse backgrounds with no excuses, requires an all hands on deck approach that benefits from a type of servant leadership and attention to emotional temperatures.

Educators and education leaders need the support of other educators to thrive. They need allies in order to truly tap into their own agency and make monumental and sustained change, even if it starts with the smallest first step, like dipping a toe in the ocean. No effective educator is an island. In fact, there is research showing that the power of collective efficacy among educators is more significantly predictive of student achievement than socioeconomic status.[51]

This idea can be summarized by the term "collective efficacy," which is both a concept and a metric that captures the sense of shared goals and a shared belief in the ability to accomplish those goals as a team of educators. Collective efficacy is a feedback loop: the more a team of educators feels that they have common (shared) goals and the more confident they are that their whole group is working toward this shared set of goals (efficacy), the higher their collective efficacy. Collective efficacy could be thought of as a type of "team agency" because it fundamentally requires a belief that the desired outcome is possible and worth striving for.

While the applications of collective efficacy seem wide-ranging, with potential applications in any group of people, whether in neighborhoods, organizations, or other institutions, the majority of research

---

[50] Reginald Green, *Practicing the Art of Leadership: A Problem-Based Approach to Implementing the Professional Standards for Educational Leaders* (Pearson, 2017).

[51] Jenni Donohoo, John Hattie, and Rachel Eells, "The Power of Collective Efficacy," *Educational Leadership* 75, no. 6 (March 2018): 40–44.

done on the subject pertains to collective efficacy in schools.[52] Repeated iterations of research on collective efficacy have shown that the higher the sense of collective efficacy, the higher the likelihood the students working with those educators are to attain academic success. In fact, John Hattie, in his extensive and impressive meta-analysis of education research, found that collective efficacy is *the strongest indicator* of student success amongst all variables studied.[53] While most educators might instinctually understand the relevance of these findings to their work striving to promote student achievement, they may also wonder, "Why does this matter in a book on educational leadership?"

Well, for one, collective efficacy cannot be sustainably built from the grassroots up. Teachers cannot simply *agree* to be collectively efficacious and then proceed forward, reaping the rewards of that efficacy. That is to say, educators themselves cannot build collective efficacy across all levels and cultures at their school, rather, *collective efficacy must be built and nurtured by the leader.* As with many things good and bad in *any* organization (especially those within the public sector), there are many entrenched levels of bureaucracy and top-down accountability making the allyship and support of equity-oriented leaders is necessary. Schools are no different and in fact, top-down accountability is on the rise.[54]

The equity-oriented educational leader stands on fertile ground for influencing and sustaining student achievement and student wellness.

---

[52] Jenni Donohoo, John Hattie, and Rachel Eells, "The Power of Collective Efficacy," *Educational Leadership* 75, no. 6 (2018): 40–44; Hattie, John. *Visible Learning: A Synthesis of Over 800 Meta-Analyses Relating to Achievement* (London: Routledge, 2010); Roger Goddard, Wayne K. Hoy, and Anita Woolfolk Hoy, "Collective Teacher Efficacy: Its Meaning, Measure, and Impact on Student Achievement," *American Educational Research Journal* 37, no. 2 (2000): 479–507Click here to enter text.; Roger Goddard, Yvonne Goddard, and Eunsook Kim, "A Theoretical and Empirical Analysis of the Roles of Instructional Leadership, Teacher Collaboration, and Collective Efficacy Beliefs in Support of Student Learning," *American Journal of Education* 121, no. 4 (2015), https://doi.org/10.1086/681925.

[53] Jenni Donohoo, Timothy O'Leary, and John Hattie, "The Design and Validation of the Enabling Conditions for Collective Teacher Efficacy Scale (EC-CTES)," *Journal of Professional Capital and Community* (2020), https://doi.org/10.1108/JPCC-08-2019-0020; John Hattie, *Visible Learning: A Synthesis of over 800 Meta-Analyses Relating to Achievement* (Routledge, 2009).

[54] Schneider and Berkshire, *A Wolf at the Schoolhouse Door.*

Great leaders of schools build agency—which in and of itself is sustaining and fulfilling. I believe developing agency is strongly tied to collective efficacy: creating the conditions for each member of the ecosystem to become stronger fortifies the whole.

We now turn our attention to hearing from educational leaders directly, through their stories that I have collected and presented for you.

Chapter Summary

Learning takes place inside of schools and outside of them but learning that occurs inside schools reflects largely what a society deems valuable for students to know. Community members thus can feel strongly about what should be taught, sometimes leading to resistance to educational leadership and restriction of ideas in schools, such as book bans and a historical accounting of the United States that omits critical parts. Schools maintain democratic processes of societies by directly shaping a community's beliefs or ideology. There is a feedback loop of sorts working between schools and society.

Although schools are a pillar in the functioning of a community, they also become a coercive element when elites exert sway over schools' social narrative. Our (capitalist) ideology often ingrains within us the belief that achievement and opportunity gaps are inevitable. Social reproduction theory argues that social order is maintained by schools, whose practices can perpetuate inequality within the schema of social structures, especially the racial achievement gap. A structuralist perspective (perhaps pessimistically) holds that social structures frame each person's destiny. But people can directly disrupt structures by using their individual agency to access resources and overcome barriers preventing positive, equitable change. The agency of students also taps into the social and cultural capital that schools provide. The achievement of all students and development of their agency depends in large part on the agency of educational leaders, who lead systems-level change. An effective leader builds agency of all stakeholders, shepherding them to becoming a team and building collective efficacy.

2

Build Better Systems
Address Students' and Stakeholders' Basic Needs

IN OUR FIRST STORY CHAPTER, we begin with the importance of setting the foundation upon which we want to work. Here, storytellers Angela Duckworth, John B. King, Noel Anderson, and Sharon Wolder remind us that to achieve relational, cultural, or structural change, we must address the environment. Working and leading in education requires developing systems and processes that can efficiently mobilize stakeholders en masse because the constraints and challenges are ubiquitous.

The consummate educational leader guides and mentors stakeholders to step into their own power so the leader is not always needed themselves. A leader who uses more authoritative leadership styles is less effective and motivating than one who develops collaboration and collectivism among constituents. A system is not functioning properly if a leader steps away for a time and upon returning finds a situation that has deteriorated.

How can a leader ensure that each person they serve is getting what they need to be their best? How can educational leaders systematize the supports they provide, but also *individualize* resources too, so that each child receives a quality education in order to be their best? In this chapter storytellers share moments when they were put to the test—and had to deliver in times of need. They relate what they learned from their experiences and how they apply those lessons when similar situations arise, and they explain the systems, processes, and mantras they've developed so that if they have to put out a fire somewhere else, everything will still be okay when they get back to their post.

Saving Starfish: How the Impact of Individual Support Adds Up
STORYTELLER: ANGELA DUCKWORTH
Psychologist and distinguished professor at the University of Pennsylvania and author of international bestseller Grit: The Power of Passion and Perseverance.[1]

At twenty-seven, Angela Duckworth left her fast-paced job as a McKinsey consultant to teach middle school math, which she says felt more like returning to something than taking a risky detour. Angela loved being around children who were learning. She mentored public school students during college, started a tuition-free tutoring program after graduation, and went on to attend Oxford to study the neuroscience of dyslexia. She felt ready to trade her workplace in a shiny Midtown skyscraper for a tired looking school on the Lower East Side of Manhattan, which had been selected as the set for a movie about an underserved community. Those experiences as a teacher gave her the insight that there was something particular about successful students, which evolved into her research on the psychology of "grit."

When she began researching grit, her samples were of relatively homogeneous groups—like West Point cadets and spelling bee champions—to keep context constant and find what separated the highest achieving individuals from the rest. Recently, Angela said she has been investigating the possibility of measuring and identifying the unquestionable needs students have, such as whether a child has a safe way to get home from school or can afford a musical instrument

---

[1] Angela Duckworth, *Grit: The Power of Passion and Perseverance* (Scribner, 2016).

that they're passionate about. She developed a necessities index for this, on which having all basic needs met would net a perfect score of ten. But kids facing obstacles related to poverty and underprivilege would score lower. "I'll tell you right now, my kids would get a ten on this scale, but I've taught a lot of kids who are not a ten and are very far from a ten," Angela says.

One of those from those early teaching days was "Kendra." Previously bright and motivated, Kendra was becoming increasingly forgetful, acting "a bit clueless," and squinting a lot at the board.

> Turns out that she didn't have glasses. So, I called [Kendra's] mom. Every time I called, her mom was sleeping and there was nobody else in the home. [Kendra] didn't know where her dad was. I'd call at 3:00 in the afternoon and [the mom] is like, "Don't call me now, I'm sleeping." I'd call her at 8:00 in the morning, "I'm sleeping." I never found out why her mom was sleeping all the time. But at one point I was like, "Is anybody going to get you glasses? Because I can't get your mom to answer the phone in a time that's good for her?" and she was like, "No."

It became clearer to Angela that Kendra lacked other basic necessities. Knowing the school didn't have funds for corrective eyewear for students, Angela took it upon herself to find a solution.

One day after school, she walked around with Kendra. They strolled into eyeglass stores and Angela said, "This little girl is in seventh grade, and she can't see the board. Can you make her a free pair of glasses?" Eventually, a boutique agreed to make Kendra glasses free of charge. Kendra's need for glasses "was completely an externality or contextual factor," Angela emphasizes. "It wasn't immediately obvious. You could have just attributed that to her being a slacker or unmotivated or not liking math." She pauses, and we share the unspoken understanding that sometimes educators, for a variety of reasons, are unable to identify the latent obstacles that hinder students' learning.

At the University of Pennsylvania, where Angela is a distinguished professor, the vast array of resources students have access to creates a more level playing field. The pandemic changed that, however, surfacing needs that went beyond differences in Wi-Fi connectivity. Angela elaborates,

I have been more intimately acquainted with my students' home situations because they're no longer on the Penn campus. They are thrust into more unequal circumstances. They're back in the chaos of their own home or back in the comfort of their own home, depending on where they are.

She learned one of her students has a bipolar mother who can be emotionally abusive and neglectful, and the student has to be home to take care of a little sister. Another student, after leaving the dormitory, could not afford to rent a suitable apartment and had to share one room with several people, one of whom contracted COVID-19. For that student, Angela booked a hotel room after contacting the university about legal issues and to confirm it would offer the student a more permanent solution. When asked whether she would have put the student up in the hotel "indefinitely," Angela interprets the word in a surprising way, relating it to her impact:

> I'm not sure that I have done a very good job of helping [students] navigate these things. You do what you can on a one-off basis. With my seventh-grader, she was 10 feet away from me, right? Then I noticed, of course, that she was squinting, right? . . . [For the] student who didn't have anywhere to live . . . I had to email Penn and make sure [booking a hotel] was even legal. If they had not resolved it the next day, I was going to have [the student] stay with me. But then, anyway, again, there's liability issues. But I think whether *indefinite* or not, it's just N of one, right?

Speaking as a scientist, Angela defines helping one student as having an N, or sample size, of 1. She postulates that perhaps the potential impact of that individualized help is limited, or hard to measure. Still, it is clear that the people she's been able to help have had various burdens lightened.

Talking about which types of support could be more "systematizeable," Angela mentions her new practice of giving her personal cell phone number to students, to be used only in necessary circumstances. To date, no students have abused the policy. "One of the big lessons from cognitive therapy is that you can't read people's minds," she says. In her class of 140 students, Angela has implanted mandatory, five-minute office hours for every student once a semester. Given her busy schedule, it has helped her identify and engage with the students struggling in their academic or personal lives or both. As head of CharacterLab, she has implemented a weekly "pulse check" survey that asks the graduate students, postdocs, and full-time research coordinators she manages questions ranging from whether the staff member understands their responsibilities to how much energy they are getting from their work. The responses are not anonymous, and there are clear trends related to morale and excitement throughout the year.

When asked if it's possible to support each student's nonacademic needs, as she did Kendra's, and whether some educational leaders (like principals or administrators who feel strapped for resources) might take issue with that, Angela responds, "What happens when you try to help an individual kid, like a starfish?" She is alluding to a popular parable of a child throwing starfish that had been washed ashore back into the ocean. An old man approaches and tells the child he is unlikely to make a difference, pointing to the thousands of other starfish stranded on the sand. The boy throws another starfish back into the water and replies that it made a difference to that one. Angela continues,

> I don't think the policy issue is that principals are breathing down teachers necks not to do it, it's just like, there's so many starfish. I think nobody was like, "Don't take the student around the neighborhood looking for free glasses." It was just like, "How many students could you possibly do that with? And what about all the other problems?" I don't have a good answer to the larger, "What are you going to do about all the other starfish?" You're right, you can't save them all. They're going to die, but not this one. And you throw it back. I hope we don't get discouraged by the number of starfish.

Even if we cannot perfectly *measure* the impact of helping an individual student, we can still prioritize, facilitate, and to an extent, systematize giving individualized attention that students and stakeholders deserve. We should also celebrate and share the stories of the educators who strive routinely to meet those needs.

Safe, but Stretched: Ripple Effects of Relationship-Based Support
STORYTELLER: JOHN B. KING JR.
Former US Secretary of Education and Chancellor of the State University of New York (SUNY)

John King often says, "Schools saved my life." Both of John's parents were educators. His mother passed away when he was only eight years old. His father struggled with undiagnosed Alzheimer's and he passed when John was twelve. School became John's haven—a place where he felt cared for and intellectually challenged.

When John eventually arrived at Harvard as an undergraduate, he already knew he wanted to do something with his life that would help others. He thought about going for a law degree after graduation, but he first wanted to gain experience directly working with people and children in need. John joined a student-led organization called the Phillips Brooks House Association, which serves over 10,000 youth and adults throughout the greater Boston area through many different social service programs.

He was most drawn to an education program where he taught civics as a volunteer teacher once a week. The member schools predominantly served low-income students of color. John's first placement was at a middle school in Dorchester, a neighborhood known for poverty and high crime rates at the time. In addition to supporting kids in their standard academic pursuits, the volunteer teachers used peer mentorship to get the kids excited about civic engagement. The hope was that these volunteer instructors would be perceived as cool and inspiring for their impressionable mentees.

John enjoyed the experience so much that he eventually started running his own summer school program in the Mission Hill neighborhood. He recruited fellow students and built a unique program model in which the college students lived among the community members in Roxbury (bordering Mission Hill) in the same housing development that most of the children came from. This helped the volunteers get to know the families incredibly well and get a more proximate and empathetic view into the kinds of hardships the children routinely experienced. John remembers vividly that the development was infested with roaches and rodents and that residents were often ignored when maintenance issues arose and appliances—stoves, heaters, showers—were not working.

John recounted many other challenges experienced by the community. He learned that even though residents constantly felt unsafe and unsecure, they seldom called the local police because of overpolicing and a high level of distrust. There was also a high rate of teenage pregnancy. One of John's female students confided to him that every other woman in her family had at least one child by the time they were her age, seventeen. John talks about the inherent value of the summer program:

> The work was in part about helping students have a sense of hope about their lives, the way teachers had done for me. And giving kids the sense that they may not *know* any lawyers but they could *be* a lawyer. There was a lot of attention of course to academic skills [in our program], but more than that, [we valued] socioemotional well-being and a vision for what could be possible. Helping students get on college campuses and think about college, helping students learn about careers and getting a sense of what might be possible for them.

John describes his relationships with Roxbury community members as "transformative." So much so that after his graduation he returned to the neighborhood to be a high school social studies teacher. He eventually became a middle school principal in the community and lived only a couple of blocks from where his summer program had been run. Being a leader in the summer program helped John develop an early perspective on the interrelated and insufficient resources available to marginalized populations, as well as what an ideal education might look like for students who have numerous unmet nonacademic needs.

Eventually, as commissioner of education in New York State, he led an investment in Clinically Rich Teacher Preparation Programs, in which one initiative was for student teachers to complete summer internships in the communities before their student-teaching placement. These future teachers would intern at health clinics or summer mentoring programs before their year-long teaching residency so that "they would be able to see their students and their families, not just through the academic lens but through a community lens," John said. During his time as US secretary of education, John also served as vice chairperson for the US Interagency Council on Homelessness. When asked to elaborate on his decision to hold that joint appointment, he says,

> I think about the connections across policy silos in people's lives... homelessness and housing security is a huge challenge in K through 12 and in higher ed. And as educators, we need to connect students to services in the community and support them through the consequences of [not having] security in their home. For some kids that may mean they don't have a place where they can do homework.

When asked whether his interconnectivity approach influenced his decision to run for governor of Maryland or whether it would influence how he would govern in that position, he added,

> When I explain to people why I decided to run for governor, I always talk about how as an educator, you see how other systems affect kids and families. The lens of the educator is to see how the policies and systems play out in people's individual lives. For example, I would say to folks, the first bill I want to sign is paid family leave... which to me is a baseline social insurance matter... Republicans and Independents have kids too. Regardless of party affiliation, it would make people's lives better.

To understand John's devotion to public service, we can probe his mantra "Schools saved my life." Was there a person he thought of when saying those words? He had a ready answer: Alan Osterweil. Mr. Osterweil was John's teacher surrounding the time of his parents' passing, from fourth through sixth grade.

> Mr. Osterweil looped with us for three years, which was unusual in New York City public schools at the time... He was my teacher when my mom passed in October of fourth grade. He was my teacher for much of the time that I was with my father. My father passed away when I was in seventh grade. [Mr. Osterweil's] class was this

incredible, loving space that was both academically engaging and rigorous. We read the *New York Times* every day in his class. We did productions of *Alice in Wonderland, Midsummer Night's Dream*—Shakespeare in elementary school . . . He was the kind of teacher where you finish a book and he's there with the next. You finish a math [unit], he's there with another that's a little more challenging. He created a classroom space that was deeply responsive to students' individual needs, but also an incredibly strong community. We did all kinds of field trips around the city, from the Museum of Natural History to seeing the ballet. He was the kind of teacher where you felt safe even while you were being stretched. He shaped how I think about teaching and the role of schools. A tremendous privilege of my life was being able to have him come to my swearing in as secretary.

Mr. Osterweil's consistent presence during the most challenging times in John's childhood was life-changing. He demonstrated to John the indelible value and effects that wholly encompassing educational experiences and caring mentorship can have on students who are striving to become their best, even among challenges. John, with his incredible professional resume, from principal to secretary of education, is himself a testament to the power of these invested approaches. Mr. Osterweil, by better understanding his students' backgrounds and their interests, was able to push them to greater heights academically. Mr. Osterweil represents a kind of educator that people remember for the rest of their lives. Life-changing teaching and learning experiences thrive on a foundation of strong, authentic relationships.

The Perfect Storm and a Yellow Sweater: Prioritizing Unity in Times of Crisis
STORYTELLER: DR. NOEL S. ANDERSON
Clinical professor of educational leadership and policy studies, New York University

In 2012, when Noel Anderson was asked to step in as interim executive director of Year Up New York (YU NY)—one of the nation's most successful workforce development programs in its largest market—he was not surprised, but he had mixed feelings. Noel was enjoying his post as YU NY's chief program officer, scaling up the national program to community colleges across fifteen cities. Being based in New York and having trained much of the staff personally, Noel was aware of and saw first-hand the problems that YU NY was experiencing. So, when the CEO, Gerald Chertavain, nudged him to step in as executive director just for a "few months" to help right the ship, Noel reluctantly agreed, aware the role was potentially undesirable due to many foreseeable pitfalls.

"What's so crazy is you don't realize how messed up things are until you get into the role," Noel says. Problems ran the gamut: the executive board wanted to know what was causing the ongoing turnover in executive directors. Corporate partners such as JP Morgan Chase complained about a lack of qualified students for their internships, which made up 60% of the YU NY revenue model, and it was essential that the program supply enough to meet the demand. Internally, a manager was bullying her direct reports, and fundraising efforts were dwindling. Not surprisingly, employee morale at YU NY was very low.

To top things off, a director role was new for Noel; he had never managed budgets closely, directly fundraised, or appeased a board. He was stepping into a new role with both national and local responsibilities and their inherent cultural tensions. "The local sites have their own way of functioning. I remember people would say, 'Oh that's national. This [local site] is not New York. This [other method] is not local.'" Noel found that "the programmatic aspect was disorganized because there was no one really orchestrating the pieces." Thus, Noel had to wear multiple hats and, with each, promote a different identity politics.

He recognized he had skill gaps, needed to learn new tactics, and was operating outside his area of expertise. Still, he had to show empathy to others' concerns while handling his own uncertainties. Noel said the main question on his mind was, "What does it take to lead with a high emotional quotient level?"

Then superstorm Hurricane Sandy hit the New York City area on October 29.

The YU NY Wall Street Office was totally flooded, requiring all activities to be temporarily relocated to Flatbush Avenue office in Brooklyn. Some staff members and students living in flooded areas were now homeless. The trauma of the events affected the mental health of some of the students (ages 18–24). The Wall Street program had to be moved into the Brooklyn office, forcing staff and students to co-mingle despite having different organizational cultures. This also meant that some of the students now had to commute to the location from the Bronx, often a 90-minute train ride. Noel had to manage a growing list of simultaneous priorities.

> We still had to hit our numbers [for revenue and internship placements]. But at the same time, the main challenge [was to make] sure that everybody was safe. I remember getting emergency funding for staff to find temporary housing, apartments for students, and pulling on our social workers to get people ready [for executing internship programs]. At the same time, I knew all eyes [were] on me because I also had to figure out how to get things going for the site. What I did know, and I learned pretty quickly, is the need, the absolute necessity, to leverage the talent around you and figure out how to get people mobilized and organized to do things to their best ability. If I didn't have that mentality, if I had to go it alone—the Robinson Crusoe approach—I would have probably failed pretty fast.

Noel leveraged everyone at his disposal—from both national and New York hubs and called on board members to help him fundraise for emergency dollars. He had to learn on the fly. He faced a crisis on seemingly every front, but he turned that to his advantage.

> There were a lot of unhappy people. I called everybody into this one room. This is right at the height of everything. . . . I [had] read somewhere that as a leader, especially when you're trying to get people motivated, colors matter. They call it impression management in corporate speak. I wore some mustard-colored sweater, like a Banana Republic sweater that I pulled out but I never really wear.

Noel led a successful meeting, replying to questions and comments from staff in an understanding tone. People were able to voice concerns and share their challenges, personal and professional. Folks started to feel like part of a team again, one weathering a literal storm. Noel and the group developed a mantra: "An empowered staff equals empowered students." At the end of the meeting, a woman came up to him. "'I appreciate what you did,' she said. I was like, 'Oh, thanks.' She was like, 'No, no, I appreciate you wearing your color. It brought my spirit up.'" Noel was encouraged that his impression management had the desired effect. "It was fascinating to see those little things like that made a difference."

Hearing that his sweater had raised a colleague's spirits, Noel realized he was on the right track in leading his team through the difficult time. Though difficulties had ranged from a bullying manager to a superstorm, he stayed focused in his leadership by putting basic needs first and being transparent about decision-making. At every meeting he and his team went over basic metrics related to admissions, retention, internship placements, revenue, development, and outcomes. This helped them have a shared, high-level understanding of needs and where energy and resources should be devoted. Having this unity of attention allowed the team to feel empowered, which slowly spread across the staff.

At the same time, not everyone needs to know *everything* about operations down to the weeds level. Noel learned to filter information so that his team could take action on what was needed without getting bogged down in every detail. A leader must tap into others' strengths but not in a way that overburdens strong team members or spreads people thin. Noel says, "As a leader, I learned how [to] pull on the things that you care about, not try to just do window dressing to look good, [and] be honest when things aren't working." The true metrics of his successful tenure, he said, were seen in the young people who began to thrive in their work placements.

Things had gone well enough for Noel to consider remaining as executive director of YU NY permanently. He had built a new culture and strengthened existing rapport with the team. The foundation was strong. He leaned toward staying in the role but eventually resumed his role at national. The sustained success of Year Up, a program whose commitment to keeping young people first serves as an exemplar for other organizations hoping to serve this same population, is in part a testament to the successes of Noel and his efforts during this critical time.

"It Was Possible to Do Both": Offering High Expectations and High Support
STORYTELLER: SHARON WOLDER
Deputy superintendent of teaching and learning, Brockton Public Schools

Sharon started her teaching career at Brockton High School, the largest high school in Massachusetts, which serves over 4,000 students. Back then, despite having much student diversity, Brockton High still felt incredibly segregated. Sharon noticed that even though students were technically grouped by their academic abilities and proficiencies, they seemed separated along racial and demographic characteristics.

The freshmen in Sharon's world history class were mostly students of color from lower-income homes and had been led to believe only a particular archetype of student was capable of achieving in their school—a profile that did not include them. The school never questioned its implicit assumptions and placed the students according to long-standing practices rooted in belief systems that were not evaluated or changed as the demographics of the school and community evolved. The students "bought into who they were based on where they were placed," Sharon says. "I spent more time having conversations [trying to get] them to see themselves differently than teaching history on some days because I wanted them to see their *place* in history and within their own life."

Their books were outdated and tattered and several grade levels below the basic ninth-grade standards. Some of the books in Sharon's class were at a *fifth*-grade reading level. Without the funding to buy more appropriately challenging materials, Sharon took matters into her own hands. "I raided the bookroom and found old AP European history books in the closet," Sharon says. "I found some old books no one was using. Only seniors took AP Euro." When Sharon returned to her classroom with the textbooks, her freshmen were bemused. They remarked on the small print and words with multiple syllables. Sharon turned the attention back onto them by asking, "What do you need to... work your way through this information?" The students paused, looked at each other, and collectively responded that they needed to be able to ask her questions... and access to dictionaries.

The students broke into working groups to decipher the text. A veteran teacher who taught in the same room after Sharon's class stopped by. He immediately asked Sharon what she and the students were doing. Sharon describes the interaction:

> I said, "What do you *mean*, what am I doing? They're in groups." I started explaining the lesson.
>
> He said, "No, I don't mean that. What are *they* doing with *those* books?"
>
> "What do you mean what are they doing with those books? They were in the closet. They were available. No one's using them. So, we are."
>
> "They can't read those."
>
> "Don't tell them that and watch," I said.

Sharon designed a lesson in which her students would read, analyze, and debate the content of the college-level textbooks—deemed too advanced for them. The lesson would build their vocabulary and comprehension. She told her colleague to come by again the next day. "He consistently showed up early for his class because he wanted to see what *my* class was doing," Sharon says. "There was part of me that was thinking, he wants to be able to say, 'I told you so.'" But the other teacher never got that opportunity. Sharon's students kept at it, working in teams to support each other. "When you give [students] access and convince them they can [do academic work], it becomes a powerful thing in a school system that only has certain [traditional] students making it."

Slowly, the students became more confident of their intelligence and abilities as learners. They saw Sharon willing to persevere with them and once they finished their assignment, they expected to be challenged again. The students continued to use the same AP textbooks for various activities over the semester, but stopped questioning whether they could navigate the information. Though initially Sharon checked in with the students multiple times, eventually they worked independently.

Today, as a deputy superintendent in the Brockton School District, Sharon looks back to this and other experiences of hers as a classroom teacher to guide her work as a leader. She says that educators often enter the field thinking they will "change the world for a child." But Sharon insists that this cannot be done unless they attempt to *understand* the student's world as it is. It's similar to lesson planning: "You can plan the lesson, but it only works if the people you're delivering it to can access it and work through it with you," she says.

According to Sharon, one of the biggest mistakes that educational professionals make is to interpret the inability of a student or colleague to grasp a lesson or address a workplace issue as a lack of appreciation for the help given them or the work done for them. "It becomes this personal affront for some people which causes them to take [the inability] personally and [even] enact disciplinary means [to solve it]," Sharon says, especially in a space that is naturally punitive, such as a school. Instead, a student's or colleagues' difficulties should be approached through communication and respect. When Sharon's colleagues told her, "Oh, the kids in my class can't do that," Sharon would reply, "But I have those *same* kids in my class. If they can do it for me, they can do it for you."

One of the hardest parts of Sharon's job has been to encourage an equity-forward culture. When Sharon took her district leadership role, she noticed it was very difficult for folks to admit they might be missing some part of the picture, especially the more seasoned they were. This is why Sharon focuses on building safety nets in teacher training programs that allow new teachers to feel comfortable not knowing how to do everything and asking for help. What helps people reach that comfort zone is having more open conversations about differences and sharing stories all along the spectrum. Sharon started her district tenure by creating opportunities for colleagues to engage with each other and learn about their varied backgrounds, cultures, and racial histories. She helped her peers grapple with the differences between equality and equity.

Sharon employed this same inclusive mindset as principal of the same school when she committed to reducing the suspensions and expulsions and leveraging interventions. Sharon wanted her staff to not only notice problematic behavior but also identify the cause before deciding the appropriate action to take.

The year after she took the principalship, Massachusetts enacted a law that loosened zero-tolerance policies. "Some people thought I made up the law, to be honest with you, and hated me for it." Some of the teachers did not want to work with "problem students" when they could simply remove them from their class. "But when you're fourteen in high school for the first time and all of a sudden you're supposed to be grown and you're a kid at the same time, you're going to make not-so-great choices," Sharon says.

Before implementing her interventionist approach, Sharon's school was a Level 1 school, the best designation for student and school achievement. Despite pushback from teachers who feared the school's classification was in danger, Sharon remained steadfast in her vision. The school reduced the number of suspensions and punitive measures and remained a Level 1 school while she was principal. Sharon did not use the standings to gloat, but did use the opportunity to "keep reminding people it was possible to do both."

Years after, Sharon took a district-level leadership position in Brockton. She began her tenure by visiting every school in the district to see whether staff and students could discuss and celebrate differences. She found that many schools lacked this capacity, and she started a district wide committee that created professional development for leaders and an equity checklist for the basics professionals needed for conversations around what equity actually means and would look like within their walls, given their student populations. She believes it is possible and should be expected to *do both* at every level. "It is possible to address behaviors, put in interventions, keep students in school, and maintain an academic status, in terms of state accountability, at the highest level."

Chapter Summary

The stories in this chapter guide us to build better systems as well as develop routine leadership practices that promote greater equity. The following are some of the main lessons from these stories that highlight this theme.

Overcome the Trap of Low Expectations

The unifying lesson from this chapter's vignettes is that *all* students have nonacademic needs that affect their academic performance.

These compound when students have social, economic, or emotional challenges, as did Angela Duckworth's student, Kendra, or John King as a young orphan. In a community-wide crisis, the brunt of burdens often falls on low-income people of color. During Hurricane Sandy's aftermath, less privileged communities and individuals were the ones most frequently displaced from their homes, leading to increased traumas and insecurities. During the COVID-19 pandemic and its aftermath, these groups similarly experienced greater rates of hospitalization and death.[2]

These social, economic, and emotional challenges are made worse when they converge and compound. Inattentive leaders might fall into a trap of diminished or deficit expectations, believing that students simply have too much to deal with to then also be given academic and professional responsibilities, or that students or constituents are lazy and don't have enough grit. Duckworth—the preeminent scholar of grit—says, when describing Kendra's eyesight or her unreachable mother, "You could have just attributed [her disengagement] to her being a slacker or unmotivated or not liking math."

To overcome these compelling fallacies, we must work to maintain high expectations for all students (and stakeholders), while also offering them high support. This is exactly what Sharon Wolder did when her colleague doubted her students could read AP European history. "Just watch," she told him. Wolder's insistence that it is possible to "do both"—address undesired behaviors *and* foster (academic) excellence—is what all equity-oriented leaders should strive for.

High expectations and high support go hand in hand. We cannot, in good faith, offer one without the other and expect improvement. Addressing behaviors without also improving the conditions in which the behaviors take place, especially during turmoil, is futile. Noel Anderson understood this when he was charged with uplifting morale at his organization following Hurricane Sandy. His first course of action was to mobilize resources for constituents to be able to get back on their feet.

---

[2] Jaclyn Kelly and Anindya Kundu, "Striving Despite Disruption: Young People's Occupational Identity and Economic Opportunity During COVID-19," in *Regional Economic Systems*, ed. Fred Olayele (Edward Elgar, 2022).

Offer High Expectations and High Support by Getting More Proximate

John King's story shows us that we can adopt the high-expectations, high-support mindset by getting more *proximate* to problems we want to solve and people we want to serve. Even research in healthcare indicates that for service deliverers to better realize the weight of the structural obstacles faced by their constituents (and their impacts on physical well-being, e.g., lead paint poisoning which damages the brain and nervous systems), they should strive to understand the spaces their constituents inhabit.[3] The same, of course, goes for education; when teachers and school leaders spend more time in the communities they serve, or get to know a little about their students' and staffs' personal lives, they become more culturally *competent*, better understanding the world outside their own.[4] As Duckworth walked around the Lower East Side with Kendra searching for eyeglasses, she started to understand much more about the girl's reality.

To learn about who students and families are requires an approach that is much more involved than leaving the school building and neighborhood as soon as the bell rings. It is critical for an education leader to become familiar with constituents' realities and underlying contexts before making decisions that affect their lives. King learned this early on, during summers living in Roxbury with students and their families, and he implemented it when he became commissioner and implemented his Clinically Rich Teacher Preparation programs and community-immersive summer internships for educators. Perhaps King first learned this through Alan Osterweil, his teacher and lifelong mentor, who made

---

[3] Johnathan Vespa, David M. Armstrong, and Lauren Medina, "Demographic Turning Points for the United States: Population Projections for 2020 to 2060," US Census Bureau, 2020, https://www.census.gov/library/publications/2020/demo/p25-1144.html.

[4] Lisa Delpit, "Lessons from Teachers," *Journal of Teacher Education* 57, no. 3 (2006), https://doi.org/10.1177/0022487105285966; Jeff Duncan-Andrade, "Gangstas, Wankstas, and Ridas: Defining, Developing, and Supporting Effective Teachers in Urban Schools," *International Journal of Qualitative Studies in Education* 20, no. 6 (2007): 617–38.

each student feel respected and valued in his class. Osterweil demonstrated that when we believe that our students and stakeholders are capable, they begin to believe it themselves. These expectations lead to students expanding their worldviews and senses of possibility.

We can also get proximate by going to the source, asking constituents about where they are and what they are dealing with. Duckworth did this by mandating pulse checks and office hours for her staff and students, and Anderson's metrics helped YU NY staff understand how they collectively felt and what they needed to prioritize. When we seek to understand our partners lives and concerns, we develop cultures of care and broaden the idea of achievement to also include well-being and fulfillment.

Lead by Example and Exhibit the Cultural Capital You Want Reciprocated

In education, seeing is often believing and sometimes, that's not a good thing. Too often, what we believe has been shaped by under-resourced environments, stressful conditions, or unsupportive professional networks. To work around unfortunate systems, we need dedicated leadership to explicitly carve out and show us a better path forward. In this chapter, each of the stories has demonstrated the power of leading by example. When educational leaders roll up their sleeves and directly partake in the work they aspire to promote, others take notice. Wolder did this in her early career, giving students material that was deemed "too challenging" for them, but convincing veteran teachers it was possible by showing them results. When he took the reins as executive director in a time of crises and ensured that everyone first had a safe place to live, Anderson achieved buy-in and collaboration from staff who were disgruntled, divided, and disheartened.

This chapter illustrates that one way to lead by example, develop common ground, and garner support is through *storytelling* and *connection*. While discussing the challenges of helping individual students, Duckworth referenced research by the psychologists Deborah Small, George Loewenstein, and Paul Slovic. They found that when solicited for donations to stop hunger in Africa, people gave twice as much when letters had individual stories of children than when they listed aggregate statistics and how many people were affected.[5] Similarly, other research finds that people are more likely to put resources and energy toward causes they feel personal connection to.[6]

Sharing stories of individual starfish helps create systems that support others who also need to be thrown into the ocean. Duckworth's comment about her helping individual students being only "an N of one" downplays her efforts; even individual stories can impact others' lives in positive and formative ways, making clearer how to help others in similar circumstances as well.

Perhaps this is what King called giving students a "sense of what might be possible for them," which can be cultivated through the smallest of our actions. Anderson's brief aside about wearing a yellow sweater is an important little detail of his story. He aptly and subtly leveraged cultural capital to uplift the spirits of others through nonverbal cues. Even in the most serious times, joy and warmth can be found in the work and in each other, even in seemingly the smallest of ways. An educational leader realizes their ability to shift the tone even when confronted by the most desperate of circumstances, such as after a natural disaster or when a teenage girl says she is surprised that she has not gotten pregnant yet. In this way, educational leaders offer themselves not only as a direct source for increasing others' capacities and sense of self, but also as an embodiment of hope and self-development.

---

[5] D. A. Small, G. Loewenstein, and P. Slovic, "Sympathy and Callousness: The Impact of Deliberative Thought on Donations to Identifiable and Statistical Victims," *Organizational Behavior and Human Decision Processes* 102, no. 2 (2007): 143–53.

[6] Diane Reyniers and Richa Bhalla, "Reluctant Altruism and Peer Pressure in Charitable Giving," *Judgment and Decision Making* 8, no. 1 (2013): 7–15.

3

Make Sense of the Nonsensical

Apply Research to Unearth and Solve Injustices

IN THESE RAPIDLY CHANGING POST-pandemic times, many unpredictable social forces permeate educational spaces and cause routine disruption. Today's educational leaders contend with social pathologies while confronting an economic landscape where the gaps between the wealthy and poor continue to grow, the rising costs of educational goods and services within the K-12 and higher education landscape, and intense and uncivilized cultural wars in which vocal minorities can hijack curricula—all while welcoming a diversifying population of students and families with limited resources, support, and cultural tools.

Determining how to overcome context-specific structural barriers and obstacles requires *investigative* approaches by leaders to devise tailored solutions that best serve their constituents and provide quality resources related to achievement and well-being for all. Leaders find themselves, many times informally, becoming researchers in order to address one-off problems on the fly. In attempts to systematize and codify research-based strategies in educational leadership graduate programs, students engage with "problems of practice" research projects and dissertations. Efforts to identify, assess, and address situational difficulties can be simply observing a real-life problem and formulating a course of action to alleviate it. But not all leaders have the time, resources, or capacity for such efforts, nor should they be expected to.

But what all educational leaders should have the chance to develop is basic research prowess: asking the right research questions, generating investigation methods, and disseminating findings. This chapter presents stories about educational leaders, many seasoned researchers by trade, applying research basics to investigate a situation. From these stories we learn what it takes to think, act, and collaborate as a scholar.

It Requires Naming It: Racial Inequity as a Symptom of Greater Forces
STORYTELLER: AMANDA LEWIS
Director, Institute for Research on Race and Public Policy and distinguished professor, University of Illinois Chicago

When Amanda Lewis started college at Brown University, she assumed she was on her way to becoming a high school chemistry teacher. That idea started to change her sophomore year, when Amanda participated in the Urban Education Semester program, designed and overseen by an anthropologist named Dr. Linda Levine at Bank Street College in New York City. The immersive training provided student-teaching experiences, introduced college students to ethnographic methods to inform their classroom observations, and offered them graduate-level education courses.

Amanda observed classes in schools in the East Harlem neighborhood of Manhattan. The school, called Central Park East Elementary School, was one of the best schools in the country *despite* being nestled in very low-income neighborhoods and serving primarily students of color. Amanda received a glimpse into what excellence looked like and what could be possible for students in resource-limited settings. She learned to notice the layers and interplay between structures and culture in school settings.

After graduating, Amanda enrolled in a prestigious, two-year teacher preparation program at the University of California, Berkeley. She chose the program, she says, because "I didn't want to do one of those programs that rush you through quickly and then put you right into the classroom. I wanted to be *good* at this. I come from four or five generations of educators."

One of the first things to stand out to Amanda about the program, however, was related to not her direct pedagogical training but the larger environmental context. Within the urban school districts where she student taught, complexities abounded in terms of racial and cultural dynamics. One of Amanda's earliest placements was in a third grade classroom in Berkeley. At this school, students were roughly equally split between white and Black students. The teacher she shadowed was an award-winning educator. Amanda asked her teacher-leader and the principal which students had more referrals—a communication between a classroom teacher who needs support with a misbehaving student and the assistant principal—so she could get a sense of which children might need extra attention. But when they listed the referred kids, Amanda noticed that they included only Black boys. Many of the students identified surprised Amanda, such as Moses, a boy who quietly sat and read books to himself, as well as Kenny, who seemed the smartest kid in the class.

Over her time in the program, as these looming, bigger-picture issues related to race, school culture, and student expectations gnawed at her, it became clearer to Amanda, who had seen children of all races and cultural backgrounds thriving in Harlem, that race was the only common factor among the "problem" students in Berkeley. "Race seemed to have these teachers betraying their values," Amanda says. For instance, the educators seemed to interpret Kenny's giftedness and boisterous nature as indicating that he needed additional disciplinary correction. He was being "treated like a second-class citizen in the school," Amanda says. Yet at the same time, all teachers would oppose the idea that race was affecting student–teacher relationships.

When Amanda reflected and wrote about what she was noticing in her weekly journals—one of the training program's requirements—she was advised to focus her attention more on her math lesson planning. Amanda didn't understand the feedback because the contextual factors "are the factors that make teaching and learning much harder than they need to be." All the while, Amanda was routinely confronted by structural obstacles in the way of engaging students. For instance, Amanda was assigned a student teaching placement in Oakland in a "sheltered

English" classroom, teaching students for whom English was a second language, which was supposedly designated for Spanish-speaking students. Yet when Amanda and her Latina graduate classmate from Berkeley showed up, they saw that most students were from non–Spanish-speaking countries like Vietnam or China, or were Black kids from the neighborhood. Essentially, this program did not come close to meeting student needs. They were not able to move forward with the lesson they had planned. The gap between promise and delivery loomed large as eventually both the English-learning program and the Oakland school's charter were disbanded.

Amanda left the Berkeley master's program after one year. Today she contends that the best teacher preparation programs are the ones like Bank Street, that encourage deep, intellectual interrogation, collaboration, and rigor, as opposed to ones that simply train novice teachers and give little attention to unpacking the surrounding context. Her formative experiences in Oakland ended up guiding many of the explicit (and sometimes uncomfortable) race-related research questions she tackled in her career. Amanda chronicled many of these stories in her first book, *Race in the Schoolyard*, which has been heralded as a luminary text on racial dynamics in schools.[1]

Others, however, linked her book to critical race theory (CRT)—a topic she does not even mention in the book. Before a faculty job interview Amanda had at a prestigious institution, someone passed out copies of a negative review of Amanda's book to the entire department before she arrived on campus. Another time, her department chair confided that her book and work put him and other white men of his generation on the defensive.

But, Amanda contends, "If you are arguing that race is a fundamental organizing principle in society, and that racism is important and it structures people's lives at every level—which is what my whole career has been about—then to understand how it works, and in order to intervene and change it, [that] requires naming it. It requires naming it in all of its manifestations and in ways that people who we work with feel implicated by."

---

[1] Amanda E. Lewis, *Race in the Schoolyard: Negotiating the Color Line in Classrooms and Communities* (Rutgers University Press, 2003).

Amanda continued in her work, understanding that she was uncovering a symptom of a larger problem, not a problem itself. With John B. Diamond, professor of sociology and educational policy at Brown, Amanda wrote the popular *Despite the Best Intentions*.[2] She advises schools and districts on racial equity while helping stakeholders realize that resistance is to be expected, especially as these conversations have broader undertones related to power and allocation of scarce resources.

Amanda says she's not motivated solely by the question "What's next?," because that can obfuscate her focus. Instead, "What's next?" is aligned with "What preceded?," because her projects are mostly guided by her values. When asked what advice she would offer educational leaders experiencing turbulence and pushback while championing for racial equity, Amanda says,

> You need courage. If you're really doing this work, someone will try to take your job away. There was a superintendent I knew who was doing great work, and there were five organized campaigns to get him fired. And you still have a mortgage. [At the same time], people are not trained to be vulnerable in their leadership. People don't often say, "I don't know how to do this." It's important to have good people around you. Your job is not to do everything, but to build community in a way to work toward change.

Today Amanda has surrounded herself with a supportive and skilled team. She is the director of the Institute for Research on Race and Public Policy, which makes space in the academy for people to partake in critically engaged scholarship as well as disseminate this type of research. The institute itself has issued reports on racial justice in Chicago, in an effort to improve the conditions of the community of which they are part. Amanda stands by the idea that good research cannot be removed from the stakeholders it involves. Rather, for research to make a difference, it must leverage and also be grounded in people's experiences in order to address lingering injustices.

---

[2] Amanda E. Lewis and John B. Diamond, *Despite the Best Intentions: How Racial Inequality Thrives in Good Schools* (Oxford University Press, 2015).

Fix Something Unfair? That's What I Do All Day: Follow the Trail of Facts
STORYTELLER: SARA GOLDRICK-RAB
Author of *Paying the Price*[3]

"That's what I do all day," says Dr. Sara Goldrick-Rab when asked to talk about a time when she endeavored to fix something unfair. "But the best thing to do is to go back to 2008." Sara was then an assistant professor of higher education at the University of Wisconsin-Madison. She and her research team embarked on a new study to understand whether a private scholarship program, called the Fund for Wisconsin Scholars, was effective in helping college students succeed. The scholarship recipients were all low-income students who were enrolled in two and four-year institutions throughout Wisconsin. During one interview at the University of Wisconsin-Milwaukee, an eighteen-year-old research participant was simply asked, "How is college going?," to which she replied "Nothing is okay. I haven't eaten in two days." Sara picks up the story:

> My graduate student doing the interview came back to me, very distressed and said, "I had no idea that this is the kind of answer I'd be getting. This person doesn't have enough money to buy food to eat. What are we going to *do*?" That was more than fourteen years ago. Now I've created a movement distinguished by its focus on finding ways to ensure that college students get a shot at a degree by having money to eat and a safe place to sleep. The path between then and now was complicated

Sara initially responded by putting on her researcher hat and asking: How could this happen? Does the student have financial aid? Why is the aid falling so short? Is she the only student going through this? The team designed a survey for students across Wisconsin. "We found out that lo and behold, yes, lots of people were in that situation. There was a problem." Sara became preoccupied with understanding why financial aid was not functioning the way it was intended to do—a topic she

---

[3] Sara Goldrick-Rab, *Paying the Price: College Costs, Financial Aid, and the Betrayal of the American Dream* (University of Chicago Press, 2016).

thoroughly tackles in her book, which covers how financial aid misunderstands and inaccurately assesses students' needs, moves too slow, and offers students loans instead of grants.

Sara slowly realized she needed to expand beyond Wisconsin. She reached out to her contacts at the Association of Community College Trustees and partnered with them to identify ten representative community colleges across seven states to survey. Their results were startling: drastic financial duress, and diminished health and wellness outcomes, was common among *all* types of low-income students. Sara and her graduate student wrote an article for the *New York Times* titled "Hungry, Homeless, and in College" about a student who faced these adversities.[4] "We showed the statistics right next to the human face," Sara says. Many people reached out to say they had also encountered this problem and wanted to do something about it. Sara continues, "That's the moment we needed. We needed, frankly, a *movement*. We needed to gather people who knew this was a thing and put this on the national agenda because nobody was talking about it."

As the number of allies grew, so did naysayers. Sara encountered resistance from a sizable and vocal faction claiming that the students were simply irresponsible and financially illiterate. "I've been laughed out of rooms," Sara says. "I've been told by a college president, 'This isn't food insecurity. This is somebody who can only afford pizza and wants to eat sushi.'... I've been told that I do research for advocacy, not research for science. I've been told that I'm overstating the problem. I'm not. I'm *understating* it." Rather than slowing down or backing off, Sara doubled down. "I believe if you've got evidence on your side, eventually you will prevail."

Determined to learn more, Sara continued to build momentum and awareness. Every year, her research team increased the breadth of their survey going from the initial sample of ten community colleges to eventually surveying students at 700 institutions. Sara created the #RealCollege campaign, which started with a conference in 2016 with attendees spanning groups of practitioners, policymakers, educators, students and other champions for students who want to create a

---

[4] Sara Goldrick-Rab and Katharine M. Broton, "Hungry, Homeless, and in College," *New York Times*, December 4, 2015.

community around making sure all students have basic needs met in higher education. After multiple conferences and countless webinars, she created the #RealCollege Curriculum to scale those professional opportunities with an online masterclass. From 2015-2021 Sara and her team published an annual report on college students' basic needs in the United States, and they democratized access to the #RealCollege survey making it freely available to institutions.

Sara also expanded the field's capacity by creating new organizations. In 2013 she founded the Hope Center for College, Community, and Justice (called the Wisconsin HOPE Lab at the University of Wisconsin-Madison, with a name change upon moving to Temple University). Under her leadership until 2022, the Hope Center conducted intervention and experimental research and directly translated that into practical and policy solutions to improve students' lives. In 2016, Sara also founded a national nonprofit, Believe in Students, to provide direct support to students nationwide in the form of emergency aid, and direct support to faculty to help them learn how to effectively assist students too. Donating her $100,000 book prize for *Paying the Price* to that cause drove significant momentum, and during the pandemic Believe in Students raised and distributed more than $2M in support.

Sara elaborates on why she takes a multifaceted approach: "I work on [effecting] structural change. Predominantly and primarily, I support the nonprofits that *support* the students. I support the colleges that *support* the students, because what I want to do is, again, change the kind of structures and policies and practices that students encounter every day because our diagnosis is that's what's causing this problem, right? It's not a lack of individual will. It's not a lack of care per se. It is a lack of care from a structural, dehumanizing perspective."

Now, Sara is focused on building capacity in other peoples' research, advocacy, and nonprofit organizations to help them learn how to address students' basic needs, and is particularly focused on addressing housing insecurity and poor health. After finding that universities were inadequate homes for innovation and human-centered scholar-activism, she left academia to work independently. This also allowed her to begin teaching at her local community college, where she puts her research into action and learns from students.

Sara is driven to fight the lingering contradiction in the United States where college is touted as important for the economy, democracy, and society at large but has barriers, "like [cutting] people off from free lunch when they graduate from high school and move onto college." Until we ask whether college is a place where students can actually learn, Sara says, college will not fulfill its social function.

"I don't believe that by the time I die, we will have eliminated food insecurity from higher education," Sara says. "But almost everybody working in higher education will know that food insecurity is a real problem or was a real problem. They will know that there are things they can do and should be doing to address it. And that's been because of work to build and broaden and inspire a movement. Even when it went well beyond anything I was comfortable with [and knew how to do] and often felt like I was flying by the seat of my pants. There are some amazing inspirational leaders out there who are doing this work too. Together, we will get this done."

Closing Schools . . . Equitably: Making Tough Decisions Where Everyone Is Heard
STORYTELLER: JOHN MALLOY
Assistant executive director, School Superintendents Association (AASA)

Before Dr. John Malloy returned to the United States to become a superintendent in California, he held a variety of positions throughout the Canadian educational system. John had been an English teacher, principal, vice principal, and even guidance counselor on his way to becoming the director of education (the Canadian equivalent of superintendent) for the Toronto District School Board, the largest school board in Canada. When asked about his experiences navigating "equity challenges," John immediately thinks back to 2009 shortly after becoming the Director of the Hamilton-Wentworth District, forty minutes west of Ontario. Things kicked into high gear when, on his first day, John learned that the board had decided to consider closing high schools in the district. Part of John's job was to oversee this process.

Hamilton-Wentworth student enrollment had been declining for some time. There were eighteen high schools, some of which had become too small to offer a wide range of programs. John explains why this threatened equity:

> We needed to think about the facilities issues that were plaguing buildings that were, in some cases, 100 years old, no exaggeration. But more importantly, what had developed over time is that some schools were perceived as the schools to get into. Other schools were perceived as the ones to run away from. Some schools became the place where kids with special education needs were sent. What you're hearing from me is [that] a whole culture had developed around these eighteen schools.

Schools with smaller populations, John says, aren't able to offer the same supports and resources as other schools because budgets become stretched too thin. The enrollment numbers indicated that having fewer high schools would increase the remaining schools' abilities to thrive. Furthermore, some of the high schools were only about fifteen minutes apart from each other, meaning that many of those students would not necessarily experience longer travel times.

John spearheaded an investigation to assess the schools' alignment with legal requirements and how well they were serving their students. He also prioritized regular engagement with the community to learn from them and ensure they knew the administration's considerations and decision-making process. Some more-advantaged parents and stakeholders, possibly feeling threatened by an overview and inventory taking that might close their school, vocally opposed the process. John says that despite these pressures he kept bringing the broader discussions back to simple questions of whether students had access to fundamentally necessary resources: What kinds of learning opportunities did kids need? What kind of social and emotional resources were required for all students to achieve? "And . . . our [assessment] leaned into the place that made people uncomfortable. How do we eradicate the have and have-not approach to our high school system in this city?"

John remembers telling the board president that he would not agree to a "typical school closure process," in which decisions are often made quickly without investigating all options or valuing the community's feelings. These kinds of closings often polarized families and led to deep community fractures. Instead, John's student-centered agenda called for honesty with stakeholders, though this honesty led to challenging public discussions and debates. He also returned to the same, simple logic that too many schools meant not enough money (for programs, athletics, etc.) to support all students within them. Even though closures were necessary, John wanted to use the occasion to acknowledge people's distress, inviting parents and others to share their feelings at meetings.

John explains what motivated his community-engaged leadership:

> I knew intuitively the kind of reactions that were going to come. I knew that because oddly enough, when I was a kid, my high school closed. I [was] a tenth grader whose school was closed. You lose your community; you lose your connections. I was one of those people screaming as a kid, "How dare you take my school away!" So, it's an odd kind of experience to be someone who's now in a leadership position, looking at school closures, even if it is from a different lens.

As a teenager in Cleveland, John was devastated by the loss of his school and the social capital that came with it. His enduring memories of the event made him sensitive to and uniquely aware of the ramifications of what he now faced. His past experience helped him be more empathetic to the families of Hamilton-Wentworth. He told them, "I understand you love our schools, and that your kids are well served here. And I don't want to take that away. However, our mandate is to support you and your kids, as well as all of our kids, some of whom aren't being supported right now."

John's team began researching who was and was not supported by the existing schema. The team collected relevant data on demographics, student achievement, student well-being and reviewed data from previous decades to find where students were being underserved. The administration was then able to show how low enrollment across schools was bad for each school and its students. John hoped to foster confidence in his goal of keeping open the schools best positioned and resourced to serve more students. John says that decisions may have been easier because of Hamilton's atypical diversity—affluent, middle-, and lower-class families often lived in the same neighborhoods. Thus, some of the most underresourced and underachieving schools had more demographic and class-based variability within them than usual.

How did John and his administration ultimately recommend which schools to close and which to keep open? The schools selected for closure weren't the lowest performing or the ones serving more students from lower socioeconomic backgrounds. Instead, the decision was based on school location and the condition of the building. Because the district could not build all new schools, they opted to keep open the buildings with the best infrastructure and the ones that could serve the most students without greatly increasing their commutes. "So," John says, "some of the schools that closed would have been perceived as fine. Others that closed were not fine."

Weathering the public perception storm required courage from John and his team as well as the school board. Research to collect perspectives and insights from stakeholders at multiple levels also aided them. In the end, they succeeded given their methodological and human-centric approach. Today, Hamilton-Wentworth has thirteen strong high schools with fairly heterogeneous student populations. The schools are able to offer greater opportunities and support for their students. This community-first model serves as an example of how to deal with a tricky and emotional process.

There's Room at the Table for All of Us: Inclusion through Community-Engaged Scientific Inquiry
STORYTELLER: PRUDENCE CARTER
Sarah and Joseph Jr. Dowling Professor of Sociology and director of the Center for the Study of Race and Ethnicity in America (CSREA) at Brown University

"It's a full circle moment," says Prudence Carter, former president of the American Sociological Association. She's thinking back thirty-plus years, to her undergraduate studies and then to her first job at

Brown University. Today, Prudence has returned to Brown as a distinguished professor, a position she recently accepted following a decorated academic career with stops as faculty at Harvard and Stanford and a deanship at the UC Berkeley School of Education. Fittingly, Brown is where Prudence's interest in sociology and inequality took root.

After college graduation, Prudence stayed at Brown for her first job as a college admissions officer. She was responsible for overseeing application processes for five states, which included two extremely wealthy areas of Massachusetts and New Jersey. The contrast between rich schools and poor schools was immediately noticeable. "I was on the road for months, traveling from center cities and urban metropolises, looking for academic gems and stars. And [in some schools] I couldn't even find the chalkboard sometimes," Prudence recalls of her trips to low-income, underresourced areas.

From those resource-depleted settings, Prudence went on to visit "some of the most idyllic [high school] campuses where students had absolutely everything." In the cold northeast winter these schools resembled the Ivy League campuses, gothic buildings with pointed arches and stone gargoyles covered in fluffy white snow.

Prudence was astonished by the extremely low student to teacher ratios at these schools and how students were offered intense but engaging academic experiences that triumphed over anything she had experienced in high school and even in many of her classes in college. As a young child, Prudence grew up in the Mississippi Delta during the late-stage civil rights and post–civil rights movements. She is a product of de facto segregated public schools as well as the child of educators.

As an admissions counselor, Prudence scoured thousands of applications to make reasoned recommendations to the admissions board. She took her position seriously, realizing that these decisions affected young people's life trajectories and earnings potential. "I learned about all the forms of affirmative action, not formalized but geographical and global representation. [The university] needed enough people in the sciences, they needed enough people to populate the various extracurriculars from the sports to the orchestra and to be in theater and arts. There were so many different permutations and combinations we were trying to do." This meant that some students could have all the "right things" on their resume and still not get in. These were unfortunate realities of the job and the process, Prudence learned.

During this period at Brown, there was also a movement to have the university adopt need-blind admissions, where students' home income levels would not affect their potential acceptance. Financial aid had previously been a large determinant in the admissions for lower-income students, where only a set number of aid-qualified students would be admitted, so such a change would ideally benefit even more deserving students with economic disadvantages.

"You would see the nexus of race and class come together," Prudence continues. "For Brown to diversify racially and ethnically, particularly for historically underrepresented groups, it would take those students. But many of those students would end up being the ones who would need more financial aid. We were reproducing and creating a high correlation between [students] who were lower-income and those who were underrepresented racially minoritized students."

In other words, before need-blind admissions became the rule, the lower-income students at Brown ended up most often also being the students of color. The wealthy students—including many legacy admissions and children of high-profile donors, "whose family's names were on the buildings"—were white and not necessarily the most academically inclined. Prudence describes realizing that lower-income white students often got the short end of the stick in these policies. "Some of the hardest cases were working-class and poor white students; unless they rose to the top in their regional pool or in an athletic pool, they had a hard time getting in."

Though only a recent college grad at the time, Prudence voiced her opinion in meetings with senior staff where acceptance and rejection decisions were being made. "We had intense sociological discussions about class, about race and ethnicity, about nativity, about stratification and higher education. It was low-paying work but it gave me time to figure out what I wanted to do." She gravitated to studying sociology and conducting research to better understand how social forces interact and affect people's lives as well as how to counterbalance these forces in educational spaces.

Prudence went on to a doctoral program at Columbia University. She quickly joined a multidisciplinary team on a research project in

Yonkers, New York, involving low-income families and students. Prudence eventually designed her own research project that would become her dissertation and her first book, *Keepin' It Real*.[5] The book immediately made a unique contribution to the field which had previously been primarily focused on explaining the underachievement of minority students through a cultural (deficit) perspective that suggested Black students often showed active disdain for academics because they associated it with selling out and "acting white." This scholarship, which Prudence directly confronted, falls under the umbrella "cultural opposition" theory largely developed by anthropologist John Ogbu, who went on to have many prominent and controversial iterations that implicitly blame students for underachievement.

Prudence, who was trained on these theories as a young scholar, says, "'I anticipated I was going to see what Ogbu was saying but I'm just not finding it . . . This is not what these kids are talking about. This is not the meaning of resistance to 'acting white' as it's been written and as I understood it.' I remember pulling out the recorder and saying that to myself." Instead, Prudence's interviews and surveys found that the most successful students savvily negotiate multiple cultural identities within rigid school systems. Rather than supporting stereotypes or stigmatizing students, she gave credit to students for this ability to navigate multiple worlds with varying expectations.

Prudence described how the students in her sample called upon many rich cultural traditions—from hip hop to Mozart—in order to thrive academically while developing their unique identity within school spaces and in the face of structural constraints. Her work indicates that to close the Black–white achievement-opportunity gap, we need to facilitate intercultural *communication* rather than assimilation. Guided by Prudence's research, a generation of scholars and practitioners now recognize and celebrate various multicultural styles, displays, and perspectives. At the same time, we understand the importance of avoiding education's rampant deficit perspectives and positioning students through more asset and strengths-based lenses.

---

[5] Prudence Carter, *Keepin' It Real: School Success Beyond Black and White* (Oxford University Press, 2005).

Upending conventional wisdom and offering a different perspective was rare, especially for junior scholars. Prudence doubled down by making her book as accessible as possible, despite it being academic in genre. "I wanted those kids to be able to pick it up if they could and decipher some of it," says Prudence of the students who participated in her study. "I wanted my parents, who were educators retiring at that time, to be able to read it. I come from a family of teachers. I was trying to speak to the practitioners as well as to academics."

Over time, Prudence naturally stepped into many leadership positions, leading large research centers, becoming chair and dean of a top school of education, and most recently being named the 2023 president of the American Sociological Association. She accepted these leadership positions with the intention of promoting her values. "Certain things have always been important to me," Prudence says. "One is that women and minoritized peoples are part of the conversation and that departments and faculty are not dominated by white men. That our voices be heard ... even as a junior, mid-career scholar, I always took a chance to speak up in meetings."

Prudence credits her keenness for advocacy to her southern heritage and upbringing. "[My siblings and I] were empowered to believe that we were equal to everyone and we could speak our voices and let our voices be heard too."

For Prudence, creating space for others' voices—especially those who have been traditionally excluded—has been a personal mission of sorts. During her deanship at the UC Berkeley School of Education, Prudence made it clear from the time of her hiring that she had an agenda to make a real-world impact:

> I only wanted to take [the deanship] if I could work with faculty who wanted their research to matter to the local community and beyond. One of my initiatives as dean was to create a strong research-practice partnership with the Oakland Unified School District so that [we] could co-construct research questions and for Oakland to draw on the expertise of the scholars and researchers at Berkeley while we drew on their expertise as practitioners, [feeding] back into how we ran our teacher ed and leadership programs.

For Prudence, the motivation to do work that matters and the desire to promote inclusion are one and the same. "There are multiple typologies of the kind of academic labor that we do. And I think that there's room at the table for all of us. But I, especially, am interested in the marriage of what I was trained to do as a social scientist with how to translate that effectively into interventions that solve social problems." In this way, Prudence is similar to many educational leaders on the whole: we endeavor to the best of our ability to solve social problems.

Chapter Summary

The stories in this chapter teach us how to recognize obstacles and devise strategies to address them. These are iterative processes and could be described as creating links between research and practice. Some main lessons from these stories that highlight this theme and how to engage it follow.

Unfavorable Causes and Effects Must Be Questioned

Both subtle justifications and complex factors are behind inequitable circumstances, especially in education. We all want children and young people to thrive, and when we seek to understand unfavorable truths—as Amanda Lewis did, in asking why certain students were sent to in-school detention at higher rates, or as John Malloy did in investigating which schools were not adequately serving students—the reasons given may not always match up with the *reality* of the situation. To find explanations, we should look beyond the surface, have conversations, make observations, and even access outside data. Only then do interesting and overlooked ideas emerge. In this way, anyone can become a researcher.

When we *stop* questioning why things happen, we are throwing up our hands in surrender to the status quo, deciding that certain, suboptimal outcomes are inevitable, when they are not. As a graduate student,

Prudence Carter diverged from the status quo when she challenged oppositional culture theory of the preeminent scholar John Ogbu. Black students she observed were not simply opposed to achievement because they resisted white norms; nay, they had more multicultural wherewithal and agency than that. And if Malloy had not used his own experience as a young student whose school was closed as a vantage point to question standard thinking for school closings, he would have simply closed "failing" and underserved schools first; the loudest and already well-served voices would have hijacked the process. Instead, by questioning the whole system, Malloy was able to institute a reasonable and equitable school closure plan. Similarly, if Sara Goldrick-Rab had not pursued a single initial thread—how a college student *with financial aid* was still going hungry and unhoused—she would not have unraveled the massive national problem of food and housing insecurity in higher education.

Sometimes, the educational leader is *not* the one who notices a thread worth following, but they do have to decide that the thread is worth pursuing. This is what Goldrick-Rab did when her graduate student came to her distraught upon learning about a research participant's severe nonacademic challenges. Though the research project, large scale and externally funded, was focused on answering other questions and topics, Godrick-Rab made the call that the team had to investigate further. Following this thread unearthed a bumpy and contentious road, but what unfolded was a lifetime of other research projects and advocacy efforts to secure basic rights for college students across the country. What transpired became a movement.

Data and Evidence Are Allies for Promoting Equity and Inclusion Despite Pushback

As a recent college grad and newly hired admissions officer, Carter traveled across the Northeast, moving between spaces characterized by extreme wealth and poverty. She noticed structural, political, and interpersonal (or relational) dynamics that influenced the quality of education for college applicants. Though Carter could not fully describe these interplays at the time, she used her informal site visits as the basis to advocate for policy change.

Carter sat at the table with more senior staff at Brown, representing the underrepresented, as she engaged in intense discussions and debates around race, class, and higher education. Advocating for others became habitual as she climbed the ranks from graduate student to dean at a large and prestigious School of Education. One has to become comfortable at addressing and managing pushback to be most effective at it.

When stakeholders and leaders come to the table armed with research and data, they are more likely to shift hearts and minds. Malloy instituted a community-minded research process to show stakeholders how the existing schema of schools left most students without resources they needed. Over time, through transparency and dialogue, Malloy received the buy-in necessary to successfully undertake his plan.

As Amanda Lewis learned, what helps more than anything is evidence: evidence that ingrained patterns, relationships, and situations are not serving all youth equitably, that these are not simply one-off, unrelated events. The research process helps us to make the case that unjust systems can and must be better. Lewis's early experiences seeing the thriving, low-income students at the Bank Street School, forged her lifelong conviction that excellence was not *only* possible for all children but necessary, and from this conviction was borne all her subsequent research. Pedro Noguera and I took Alabaman educators to thriving schools serving diverse students in New York City, a story I recount in the introduction, and they started to believe in the possibility of success for all as well. Sometimes, research is more impactful if it focuses on what works instead of focusing on why things are broken.

Shifting attention and energy to believe in the potential of all students sometimes requires some unlearning. The ideas of the storytellers in this chapter were opposed. Leaders, especially those who pursue and advocate for equity, must understand that taking less-traveled paths is not always easy or supported. Goldrick-Rab lost former allies. She endured administrators in her field who discredited her findings and called her research unscientific. Still, she knew that she had stumbled upon something undeniable that she couldn't ignore. She stayed the course and picked up new partners who aligned with her emerging values and perspectives while creating a more expansive national network.

Collaborative Research Is Powerful, Sustaining, and Systems-Changing

Researching and challenging entrenched structural barriers requires deliberate and methodical efforts over long periods. Fighting these fights requires determination, stamina, and a positive outlook. Because these mental resources are finite, they are easily exhaustible. Thus, it becomes absolutely critical that educational leaders surround themselves with like-minded peers, collaborators, and direct reports who fuel their fire. Carter's adage that there is "room at the table for all of us" signals not something "nice to have" but an essential asset: collaboration in research is a *must*.

When research is backed by an alliance of individuals, different strengths and abilities emerge, positioned to make lasting social change. Collaborations and relationships can last and help develop our interests; they do not necessarily need a formal capacity to have an effect on us. When Amanda Lewis learned ethnographic methods from Dr. Levine in college, she carried those lessons with her throughout her life across locales and projects. As a graduate student at Berkeley, Amanda developed solidarity with the only two minority female graduate students in her program. They too critically saw the program's peculiarities in a similar light.

Educational leaders have to secure resources and opportunities to build their teams how they see fit, as Goldrick-Rab did, over the years, establishing teams and research centers around her newfound mission of ending housing and food insecurity in higher education. Other times, we can build capacity where we are rooted, as Prudence Carter aimed to do as Dean at the Berkeley GSE. Her first endeavor was to catalyze the creation of research-practice partnerships between her faculty and the Oakland Unified School District so they would co-construct research questions and subsequent plans for answering them.

Sometimes, a leader must spend time on the ground among constituents and stakeholders to identify emerging needs. This is what John Malloy did as newly appointed superintendent. Malloy not only had a team of researchers at his command at the district, but also strategically built grassroots support, subtly enlisting parents and other community members to share their grievances and inventory their sentiments, making them feel a part of the research process and overall mission to better serve all students.

One thing is clear: educational leaders are primed to generate shared opportunities for investigation and improvement among communities. Research can be one of many methods to open doors to greater inclusivity.

4

Stick to Your Guns

Lead with Values, Conviction, and Information

CO-AUTHORED WITH JASON LE-RESELOSA, DOCTORAL CANDIDATE, NEW YORK UNIVERSITY, SOCIOLOGY OF EDUCATION CHAPTER

To make meaningful change, leaders must remain steadfast in the face of adversity. Inevitably at some point, we have and will become daunted by an uncontrollable situation to which we feel trapped. Perhaps you're driving during rush hour, late to an important meeting, but all you see in front of you are a sea of red brake lights, bumper to bumper for miles. Or imagine, more relevantly to this exploration, that you were a prominent education policy influencer, but you have a significant change of policy views in the later stages of your career. Now your former allies work tirelessly and publicly to strike you down. How would you find the freedom and courage to persist on this new terrain? Most people might say that paying those kinds of prices is not worth the cause, but luckily for us, the best educational leaders are not *most* people.

In US history, one figure stands out for embodying this type of resilience: W. E. B. Du Bois, the first Black person to earn a doctorate degree from Harvard University and a prolific writer. Du Bois is often mischaracterized as merely a literary figure. In actuality, he is a founding father of American sociology who maintained unwavering conviction in the face of opposition.

Du Bois was commissioned by the University of Pennsylvania to more or less answer the question: What is wrong with the "Philadelphia Negro" and why can't they advance themselves in society? In answer, Du Bois produced in 1889 his signature sociological and epidemiological study of African Americans in Philadelphia, *The Philadelphia Negro*.[1] The study, a form of advocacy and leadership, educating a racist society that racism exists, was systematically marginalized within the canon of sociology, dismissed by elitist white scholars who rejected his work as biased by an insider's perspective.[2] Du Bois responded to his critics by saying, "So far as the American world of science and letters was concerned, we never 'belonged'; we remained unrecognized in learned societies and academic groups. We rated merely as Negroes studying Negroes, and after all, what had Negroes to do with America or science?"[3]

As we learned in Chapter 3, the most effective educational leaders study their communities to find how to help them; being part of the in-group—sharing its sentiments and solidarity—is what gives them their important vantage point and edge. Du Bois resiliently continued his scholarship to promote racial equality and educate others on the plight of Black Americans.

In his study of African Americans in Philadelphia, Du Bois compared the everyday lives of white Americans and Black Americans, even going door to door to ask families about their livelihoods. He learned about people's backgrounds, education, work experience, criminal history, families, health conditions, and more. He collected data from over nine thousand African Americans. In the end, Du Bois answered the question he was asked but flipped it. He directly showed that Black Philadelphians could not advance and suffered worse life outcomes

---

[1] W. E. B. Du Bois, *The Philadelphia Negro: A Social Study* (University of Pennsylvania Press, 1889).

[2] Christopher White and Matthew W. Hughey, "Above the Color Line: WEB Du Bois's Otherworldly Perspective and a New Racial Order," *Journal of the American Academy of Religion* 91, no. 3 (2023): 605–20.

[3] Robert W. Williams, "The Early Social Science of WEB Du Bois," *Du Bois Review: Social Science Research on Race* 3, no. 2 (2006): 365–94; William Edward Burghardt Du Bois, *The Autobiography of WEB DuBois* (Diasporic Africa Press, 2013), Chapter XIII, 228.

than their white neighbors—including health disparities, occupational hazards, and illiteracy—because they lacked access to quality institutions, including education.

Du Bois's legacy is a testament to studying, addressing, and working within spaces and problems that matter to us personally—those we have an active stake in improving—regardless of opposition. Had Du Bois given in to the social pressures of the time, perhaps pursuing a less necessary line of work, he would not have advanced our understanding of race relations in the US as he did; his contributions have provided a foundation for contemporary theories including critical race theory to take root.

In this chapter, we dive deeper into the minds of educational leaders who persevered in upholding their values and convictions despite immense pressures to desist. In the stories that follow, we learn how resilience develops and promotes the agency of leaders and their constituents. Without the leadership of fringe radicals like Du Bois, US history would have stagnated. The exceptional individuals who critically defy the status quo and its expectations are why we are at all able to strive toward living up to our democratic ideals.

Soul Searching: Finding Solace in Changing Perspectives and Ruffling Feathers
STORYTELLER: DIANE RAVITCH
Author, historian of education; former US Assistant Secretary of Education

Diane Ravitch's body of work does not need much of an introduction to those who follow topics in education. Her books *The Death and Life of the Great American School System* and *Reign of Error* were both best sellers.[4] Diane's blog, DianeRavitch.net, has a large following, collecting over 42 million views as of June 2024. Despite her fame, some may not know that these books and her blog reflect a perspective that shifted monumentally from earlier in her career over what approaches are best

---

[4] Diane Ravitch, *The Death and Life of the Great American School System: How Testing and Choice Undermine Education* (Basic Books, 2010) and *Reign of Error: The Hoax of the Privatization Movement* (Knopf, 2013).

for public schools. As Diane says, she had a "dramatic change of mind and change of heart."

Before 2007, Diane had been a prominent voice and leader of the conservative movement in education, championing free-market policies for explicit standards, strict accountability for students and teachers for performance, merit-based pay for teachers, and expansion of charter schools to foster competition. But between 2007 and 2009, Diane slowly started to rethink these policies promoting competition, questioning how well they functioned in school systems and whether they or their outcomes were fair. She eventually arrived at the realization that she had been wrong in her former beliefs. In *The Death and Life of the Great American School System* she described her transformation in thinking and was publicly candid about her new viewpoints. She ended up losing much of her existing social-professional network and many close friends.

Originally, Diane had believed in the principles of meritocracy—that the best, brightest, and most hard-working climb to the top. Her own education vindicated these beliefs.

> I believed tests showed which students were the best and the most deserving. In retrospect, I think my belief in testing was grounded in the fact that I always aced tests. Those who received the highest scores deserved rewards and special treatment. I'm one of eight children, and the tests set me apart. They allowed me to go from an ordinary comprehensive public high school to an elite private college.[5]

In 1983 Diane formed the Educational Excellence Network with Chester Finn Jr., a professor, education policy analyst, and former Assistant Secretary of Education. The network distributed a monthly newsletter and other resources and supported high-stakes standardized testing, rigorous standards, and rewards for achievement. It established a strong community around the country for like-minded education professionals.

---

[5] Diane Ravitch, *The Death and Life of the Great American School System: How Testing and Choice Are Undermining Education* (Basic Books, 2016).

In 2002, the George W. Bush administration's No Child Left Behind (NCLB) law took effect. It set federal standards for testing and accountability and authorized school choice. Intended to increase achievement by poor and minority students, the law, data showed, continued large disparities in achievement between minority and nonminority students in schools that implemented its requirements.

For a few years Diane promoted the NCLB, but she kept seeing reports, news, and events that gnawed at her sensibilities. "Fast-buck tutoring companies," as Diane calls them, received federal funding. Charter schools all over the country failed and closed. Mayor Michael Bloomberg's aggressive testing and accountability strategy in New York City closed dozens of schools that served the most vulnerable and low-income students. No-excuses charter schools took their place and touted increased graduation rates citywide, while often removing the lowest performing students for behavioral issues while neglecting to address their unmet underlying academic and nonacademic needs. Diane attended a conference held by the American Enterprise Institute five years after NCLB was instituted where dozens of research papers indicated the program had been a failure. She started to suspect that many of the school policies she advocated were part of this broken paradigm.

Diane met quarterly with other prominent conservatives as part of the K-12 Education Koret Task Force of the Hoover Institution at Stanford University. They collaborated and wrote papers about practices that supposedly raised test scores, lowered underachievement, and reduced poverty. In 2008 the group met to debate how to fix NCLB, but Diane now saw its premises and mandates as flawed: "I stopped believing in the strategies of testing, accountability, incentives, and choice." The other task force members disagreed and released a pamphlet on repairing NCLB that excluded Diane's dissent. In 2009, to the surprise of her peers, Diane resigned from the Koret Task Force.

"When my book came out the next year, I was a pariah on the right," Diane said. Someone set up a fake Twitter account called "Old Diane Ravitch," mocking her for changing her views. Diane asked her old friend Chester Finn if he would write a blurb endorsing her latest book but he declined. "What had once been a close friendship dissolved. That was the saddest of all the responses," Diane admitted. After she wrote two more books critical of her past educational stances, she said,

My break with my former allies on the right was complete. Changing my mind and admitting it in public were difficult. It's not easy to leave and reject a world in which I was once very comfortable. I did it because I had to. I could not pretend to believe in ideas that I believed had been tried and failed.

Diane was no stranger to closed doors due to her politics. Teachers College of Columbia University, where she had been an adjunct for fifteen years, denied renewing her an adjunct professorship, the implication being that she was not wanted given her post in George H. W. Bush's Republican administration.

When *Death and Life* was published, Diane thought the right, especially wealthy elites, might react negatively:

> I was initially worried about the reaction from the billionaires. I thought of a Monty Python figure—a giant boot—landing on me, but it didn't happen. Mostly they ignored me. Bill Gates did say in an interview for *Newsweek* that I was his biggest adversary, which made me laugh. The solace came from the astonishing number of teachers who read my book or saw my interviews. I lost my social-political network, but gained my soul.

Diane's network started to expand as she was invited to speak by universities and conferences all over the country. But she found herself being shunned once again. "I got blackballed for having worked in a Republican administration, then again for switching sides away from them," she says lightheartedly. She was fired from an unpaid post as senior fellow at Brookings Institution in DC because of her newfound progressivism. But Diane continued to march forward, guided by her new values. She founded the Network for Public Education to advocate for public schools and teachers through equity-minded policies, and it is still going strong under Diane's leadership.

When asked if she has any systems or mantras to motivate herself despite receiving backlash and even vitriol, Diane says, "Not really," but then continues,

> I'm eighty-six. I know my time is running out. I have no ambitions other than to stay healthy and active. Because of my age, I have no

fears other than for my loved ones. I can afford to speak what I believe without worrying about offending anyone. I read widely for my blog and I post something daily, sometimes several times a day. I speak my mind. I advocate for democracy, public schools, teachers, the joy of play, and unions—which provide a path into the middle class and security for the middle class—community schools, and separation of church and state. I speak out against greed, grift, privatization of schools, high-stakes testing, misuse of technology [replacing teachers with screens], and invasions of student privacy. We should all live by the mantra, "At least do no harm."

Wrongly Convicted and yet Unwavering in Conviction: The Pursuit of Justice
STORYTELLER: SHANI ROBINSON
Former elementary school educator and coauthor of the book
None of the Above[6]

People who have directly experienced our criminal justice system often suffer unimaginable trauma. Their personal finances, relationships, and even hope may collapse during imprisonment. They may form strong resentment toward the system at large. But some manage to maintain their sense of self, even leveraging their experiences to push back against an unjust status quo. That is the triumphant choice Shani Robinson routinely makes.

Inspired by her educator mother, Shani joined Teach For America (TFA). She taught first grade in Atlanta for two years, and taught fifth grade an additional year before transitioning into the counseling field. Although she questioned TFA's role in a burgeoning corporate education reform movement—she fell in love with the art of teaching.

However, the ushering in of high-stakes policies such as No Child Left Behind (NCLB) in the 2000s gravely affected the educational

---

[6] Shani Robinson and Anna Simonton, *None of the Above: The Untold Story of the Atlanta Public Schools Cheating Scandal, Corporate Greed, and the Criminalization of Educators* (Beacon, 2019).

ecosystem. Teachers found themselves up against unreasonable expectations with little to no support. NCLB's goal was that all students gain proficiency in reading and math by 2014. Standardized tests were administered in grades three through eight, and school and district funding was tied to test scores. Test scores also affected teacher bonuses and evaluations, as well as their job satisfaction and retention. Achieving these scores came at the cost of centrally important aspects of pedagogy.

Proponents of NCLB (including, at the time, Diane Ravitch, in the preceding story) hoped these tests would lessen racial disparities in achievement outcomes, but they overlooked the effect on students' test-taking abilities from structural inequities, such as food insecurity, differences in learning styles, and cultural differences. For Shani, this meant she had to narrowly focus on test-based outcomes while teaching in a drastically underserved and underresourced environment.

Curiously, though Atlanta Public Schools (APS) set higher target goals than the rest of Georgia, its test scores steadily increased over time, despite Atlanta being fraught with race- and class-based inequities, as are most urban metropolitan areas in the US. As the test scores increased, so did allegations of cheating. Then news broke that some Atlanta teachers had altered answers on their students' tests and that others were encouraged to do so. The Georgia Bureau of Investigation (GBI) became involved and questioned Atlanta educators, many of whom did not have attorneys present. GBI Investigators were intimidating during interviews and teachers were unknowingly stripped of their constitutional right to counsel and their right to remain silent.

The Atlanta cheating scandal became the most expensive and unprecedented trial in Georgia history. Thirty-five educators were arrested. Thirty-four were Black. Many of them lost their licenses and faced misdemeanor charges. Shani had little reason to be among the group. Her first graders' test scores did not count toward the district's testing goals called "targets," and she received no bonus because of the improved test scores. But in order to receive immunity and avoid prison time, a colleague had accused Shani of being part of the cheating scandal.

Shani was charged, the youngest defendant among the bunch. She refused to plead guilty. The trial lasted eight months. Shani was even offered a deal: she could confess or turn someone else in, in order for all charges against her to be dropped. She refused.

In 2015, Shani was convicted. She was sentenced to spend one year in prison, four years on probation, to pay a $1,000 fine, and perform 1,000 hours of community service. Following this conviction, among eight others Shani appealed the decision, a process which took nearly a decade to resolve. In June of 2024, a judge deemed that the appellants could avoid prison time if they apologized for their roles in the scandal. The sentence still includes three years of probation, community service, and paying a fine. Shani is relieved that this chapter is closed.

In the original case, many co-defendants of Shani's faced financial ruin due to legal fees. They lost their teaching licenses; some lost their homes, health, and marriages. But I tell this story because of how Shani managed the aftermath of this injustice, not the injustice itself.

Shani realized she should speak up to both clear her name and expose the ills of the educational system.

Shani co-authored an illuminating and powerful book with a local journalist, Anna Simonton, *None of the Above: The Untold Story of the Atlanta Public Schools Cheating Scandal, Corporate Greed and the Criminalization of Educators*. The authors ask: Who is accountable and what can be done to improve the system? Through interviews and meticulous research, they document how Black educators, and those serving in disinvested communities, pay the price for a system that was set up to fail. Many schools and students must contend with violence, destruction of public housing, and gentrification, but the system does little to help. Teaching to the test and taking a one-size-fits-all approach not only stifles the creativity of teachers and students but lacks evidence that they benefit students. The challenges educators experience compound and the profession becomes more devalued.

The cycle continues.

Shani encourages educators to advocate for justice but also protect themselves. She recommends that educators maintain paper trails or have witnesses present during audit-like conversations. She advises teachers to seek mentors among veteran educators and discover grassroots organizations that can champion them. "My story was able to connect the dots for a lot of people," Shani says, another example of a personal narrative that sheds light on injustices in education.

Shani knows teachers must be both educators and social workers. As a teacher, Shani provided food and clothing for her students. Once, she even convinced a couple to take in one of her students as a foster child. Unity and collective action—in neighborhoods and educational communities—can and do usher in progressive change. Educators alone cannot fix a broken system and should not take the blame for its failures, either.

Despite her ordeal, Shani remains passionate about education, encouraging people to go into teaching and, with her husband, founding a nonprofit organization that helps teenagers find constructive pathways after high school.

Shani Robinson exemplifies the unbreakable determination of teachers who influence their students' lives despite overwhelming challenges. Her story, along with her tireless advocacy, calls us to action, propelling us toward a future where every child has access to an equitable and empowering education and teachers are heralded for their true value. Importantly, from Shani we also learn that we have to stand up for ourselves when no one else will. In those times, when self-doubt could take over, only a strong will can endure to promote positive social change through renewed perspectives.

Stepping Down to Take a Stand: Resignation as an Act of Resistance and Disruption
STORYTELLER: PEDRO NOGUERA
Dean of the Rossier School of Education, University of Southern California

Dr. Pedro Noguera is one of the nation's leading experts on issues surrounding the achievement gap and inequalities within public education. Pedro has amassed a lifetime of experiences in various advisory and practice-facing roles, applying his scholarly perspectives to advance access to opportunities for students with diverse needs. Nine years into a professorship at New York University (NYU), Pedro was appointed by the governor as a trustee for the State University of New York (SUNY) and served from around 2011 to 2014. In this role, Pedro chaired the Charter School Authorization Committee.

The New York City Department of Education and the SUNY Board, the only two authorizing bodies for charter schools across New York State, reviewed charter applications, which presented detailed plans for opening a school, as well as the justifications for being granted a designation as a charter school—an institution less beholden to the regulations of government-run schools. Charter schools' performance and financial results are reevaluated every few years to determine whether their charter should be renewed.

The reauthorization of an all-girls charter school on the Lower East Side of Manhattan came before the board. "And originally," Pedro says, "I supported it because it seemed like it was a good school, serving girls of color."

> But then I realized two things: they had located this school in the same building that previously was a school that served kids living in the projects on the Lower East Side. In effect, they were taking a school from *those* kids and giving it to *these other* kids. And then it turned out that most of the girls who attended this school were fairly middle-class. Their parents drove them there, they didn't have to rely on public transportation, and they were better off than the kids in the projects. So, the question was, "Why did they deserve that building more than the kids who historically had it?"

During his twelve years in office, New York mayor Michael Bloomberg's administration closed more than 200 public schools and, in their place, opened up new, smaller schools, many of them charters. The all-girls charter school that Pedro describes here was a part of this break-up and shake-up strategy, which boasted higher graduation rates over time, but likely also displaced students.

For example, in the same building that housed the all-girls charter school, Pedro says, another school served students with special needs, some with severe disabilities. If the girls' school lost its charter, the special needs school and students would be forced to relocate as well. "I expressed my concerns about that," Pedro says, "but [I learned] that as a charter-authorizer, you have no say over the location of the school and others in the building. You only have a say over the [specific] charter and its merits." This simple yay or nay process meant that a trustee could not control the other consequences of authorization decisions, including potentially harmful outcomes for other schools and students around them. This case made clear to Pedro that the board could not consider nuances and contextual factors—the larger, social picture—necessary for thorough decisions. Charter school authorization could have unintended effects.

> I can't just look at the charter and not think about the implications of . . . [our decision]. And so, I did a very public resignation, which got published.[7] I explained how charters were being used. [This case] exposed the way decisions about real estate, and who had access to it, were becoming equity issues impacting students. It tended to be that charter schools were displacing schools serving in many cases the most disadvantaged kids.

In other words, issuing a charter could have deleterious outcomes for other schools and trustees couldn't factor that into their decision. Compounding this problem of decisions with unfair results is that, as Pedro addressed in his op-ed,

> I talked about the fact that many charter schools served kids of color, but their whole boards that were overseeing them were white. They usually had members from hedge funds and large banks that had nothing to do with the communities that were being served.

Those with more proximity to the communities served and who better understand the schools' strengths and needs should oversee schools, not powerful business interests without direct relation to children's education. In education, the stakes are too high.

Bloomberg's mission to close large New York City schools and create new, smaller schools within the same buildings increased competition among hopeful school creators. As bidders competed for access to new school spaces—sometimes four or more schools were made in place of where there had been just one—surrounding communities often could

---

[7] Lisa Fleisher, "SUNY Official Resigns over Charter Issue," *Wall Street Journal*, February 2, 2012, https://www.wsj.com/articles/SB10001424052970204652904577197550308368954; Pedro Noguera, "Why I Resigned from the SUNY Board of Trustees," NPR, February 6, 2012, https://www.wnyc.org/story/303223-why-i-resigned-from-the-suny-board-of-trustees/.

not navigate the complex bidding process. Students in communities unable to enter bids were deprived of having a local school.

During his tenure as trustee, Pedro visited many of the NYC schools that he was assigned to evaluate. This is how he came to learn of the different challenges facing the schools occupying the same building on the Lower East Side as the all-girls school. He lamented not being able to visit schools in towns like Buffalo or Rochester. He was sure that systemic changes were necessary if charter schools were going to make equitable social changes they often touted in their applications. This led Pedro to ultimately decide he could have more influence from the outside, leading to his decision to resign. When asked if the choice to leave SUNY was a hard one, Pedro said:

> Yeah. I really liked the staff. When I first expressed my reservations to them, they understood. Then I told the other trustees what my concerns were. And then I even had a call with the governor at the time about what was going on, and the governor made it clear that [the current arrangement] is what they wanted to do, and they were not interested in my concerns.

During his trusteeship, Pedro observed that those closer to school administration, such as the SUNY staff, were more cognizant of (and more motivated to address) the equity deficiencies within the system than those at the top, including the governor who appointed him. "I think for the politicians it was just a blip on the screen," Pedro says.

Despite these revelations, Pedro did not wholly reject the charter school approach. He felt that he had contributed to many deserving schools' authorizations and thereby positively affected many students' and families' opportunities. The experience is "one of the reasons why my position around charter schools is more nuanced than [others']," Pedro says.

> I reject the dichotomy, the "for or against." But my willingness to publicly resign is part of who I am. I'm not willing to be used for political purposes. A lot of times academics don't want to get involved... You have to be careful that you're not being used, but you also have to be careful about how you engage in the political process because you can get hurt along the way.

Pedro's resignation came at a critical juncture. Powerful politicians at the time, including Mayor Bloomberg and incoming governor Andrew Cuomo, said during election campaigns they were pro-charter. Though Pedro's resignation may have been just a blip to some in power, to many others across the country, it was a brave, necessary deed for the sake of students.

Asian Enough: Liberating Identity Through Mental Health Advocacy
STORYTELLER: OLIVIA MOK
AANHPI student activist and youth leader

Within our racialized society today, Asian Americans continuously succumb to the effects of the "model minority" myth, which monolithically places Asian Americans onto one shared pedestal, assuming that all Asians are afforded academic opportunities which they take advantage of through hard work and talent. Relatedly, Asian Americans are finding themselves increasingly left out of discourse surrounding the oppression and inequality of minoritized peoples. More recently, this racial lumping has exacerbated a wave of hate and violence correlated with rising anti-Asian sentiments in the US, which increased during and following the peak of the COVID-19 outbreak.

Fueled by former President Trump's animosity of using anti-Chinese language and linking the consequences of the Coronavirus as the direct fault of the Chinese community, anti-Asian violence has spread to a new "yellow peril"—a stereotypical imagery of anti-Asian fear mongering—that has negatively impacted the image of the Asian American community nationwide. One Asian American student in New York is advocating to disprove myths against Asian communities, specifically striving to increase mental health advocacy and accessibility for Asian American, Native Hawaiian, and Pacific Islander (AANHPI) communities. Her name is Olivia Mok.

Olivia's passion for advocacy stemmed from her own mental health journey, which was most notably troubling during the COVID-19 pandemic. Olivia was in eighth grade when schools across the nation started switching to remote modalities. Her mental health waned as she completed middle school and started high school in isolation. Olivia recalls, "Being alone with my thoughts for so long, I dug myself into a hole and had minor depressive episodes." Olivia's high school did not provide adequate mental health support for students during and after the pandemic. For one, the school had a scarce number of counselors, preventing each student from receiving individualized attention and care pertaining to their wellness.

Olivia found herself ill-supported to manage and confront the new waves of anti-Asian violence she encountered. So, in her junior year, she participated in the AAPI-LEAD Youth Conference, which she learned about in a school-wide email from the school librarian. This conference was a beacon of light amidst a sea of hurt and hate for Olivia, as she engaged with empowering ideas of social activism. Here, she was inspired to apply to join the conference's organizer, the Asian American Student Advocacy Project (ASAP), a youth leadership program composed of AANHPI students across New York City that each year focuses on empowerment through community building and advocacy. ASAP is also a part of the Coalition for Asian American Children and Families (CACF), the nation's only pan-Asian children and families' advocacy organization. For her senior year of high school, Olivia was selected to join the 2023 ASAP cohort.

There she found a support system, particularly within the mental health committee that she was a part of. By working collaboratively and bonding over the course of the year, fellow team members and program coordinators became Olivia's greatest allies. They helped her prepare to bring their discussions from the program level to larger-scale opportunities.

At her second AAPI-LEAD Youth Conference, Olivia facilitated a workshop about equality, equity, and justice, explaining the differences between them and using data backed examples of discrepancies in the amount of support different AANHPI ethnicity groups need and receive. For example, in terms of educational access, the number of Southeast Asian Americans obtaining a bachelor's degree or higher is disproportionately low compared to the 25.9% national average (Hmong, 7.5%; Cambodian, 9.2%; Lao, 7.7%; and Vietnamese, 19.4%)[8] and are more likely to need more financial support than their East Asian counterparts (e.g., Japan, China, Korea). Olivia explains that

---

[8] Y. K. Pak, D. C. Maramba, and X. J. Hernandez, eds., *Asian Americans in Higher Education: Charting New Realities* (Wiley, 2014).

identifying these discrepancies and disaggregating this data is an important step toward building equitable support for everyone: "When it comes to equality, you can give everyone the same amount of support, but that won't help as much if someone else needs *more* of that support. In terms of equity, you're giving people the amount of support that they need [specifically] based on their socioeconomic standing and other factors."

Olivia applied her AANHPI conference experience to make an impact beyond the ASAP community throughout her senior year of high school. She facilitated a workshop at her high school, where she emphasized the diversity within the AANHPI community. Then, in spring 2024, with ASAP allies right by her side, Olivia testified with a newfound confidence and voice before the Committee on Education for the Fiscal Year 2025 Preliminary Budget Hearing, an event chalk full of New York City's political bigwigs. Here, she shared her own mental health journey as she advocated for more strategically tailored allocation of mental health resources across NYC public schools. She addressed the room saying:

> Schools [are] supposed to be places where students can thrive socially and emotionally. But due to systemic challenges and barriers, the sense of insecurity and urgency schools have created has led AANHPI students to believe that our grades are the only things that matter and that we are just numbers . . . The COVID-19 relief fund allowed 450 new social workers to be hired across all NYC schools, which is certainly progress, but still not enough . . . I would like to advocate for our youth to have what I did not have in my early education years: a true sense of support. We need the city to listen and care, not listen and cut.

Olivia's testimony reveals a key point blocking progress: though few people directly oppose ideas about equitably providing mental health support, the fact that there still persists a lack of mental health resources demonstrates the stronghold of systemic structures and, therefore, the necessity for us to do more to promote equity.

Through ASAP, Olivia gained an appreciation for the art of public speaking, learning to articulate her ideas with conviction. Finding her voice allowed her to embrace her place within the AANHPI community. Having grown up in a predominantly white neighborhood, not having many AANHPI friends in her early years, and not speaking her native language (although she is learning it right now), Olivia recalls originally not feeling "Asian enough" when entering ASAP.

This erasure of identity—being pulled by tensions to assimilate but also be authentic—is in itself a function of white supremacy felt by minoritized individuals across the US. However, throughout the year, Olivia realized that these factors do not make her less than, but only provide her room to grow and learn more about her culture. She knows now that she is "as much of an AANHPI community member as the next person."

Passionate about activism and social justice, Olivia continues to be a student activist and youth leader in her first year of college as she majors in sociology at Syracuse University. Olivia is interested in learning more about the interplay between social structures and race, sexuality, socioeconomic class, as well as other factors we inherit at birth. While navigating another predominantly white institution, Olivia commits to embracing her Asian identity, better understanding her burgeoning role as a contributor to society and empowering the AANHPI community at-large.

History Will *Not* Repeat Itself: A Mother's Advocacy
STORYTELLER:
Parent, Indianapolis

Denise grew up during the era of public school desegregation, attending elementary school in Indianapolis where all her teachers and classmates were Black. Denise loved school and felt a sense of community there. But in fourth grade, Denise and her classmates were bussed to schools in predominantly white townships, sometimes more than an hour away. Denise vividly remembers the first day she entered her new elementary school as a newly desegregated student:

> A white student came up to me and looked behind me. She exclaimed, "Where's your tail?" I said, "What do you mean by 'my *tail*?" To which she said, "Well, my grandmother said Black people have tails like dogs." I was ten years old. I went home that day very nervous about what [lay] ahead.

This was the start of a dichotomy that characterized the rest of Denise's early schooling. In elementary and middle school, Denise felt a mix of fluttering self-confidence and self-doubt. Her confidence had been nurtured by her former Black elementary school teachers and her Black neighborhood before integration. Her budding self-doubt was fostered by her new schools' explicit and implicit messages that she was not smart enough and that she did not belong. Denise sustained her motivation and well-being by becoming a student athlete and reminding herself that her family deeply valued education, which was a sentiment shared by many Black families who had historically been denied these opportunities.

Interestingly, Denise says, most of the township schools in Indianapolis that had been mandated to desegregate in the 1970s have now reversed their demographics. They are part of the new landscape of US public education, one where schools today are more segregated than before *Brown v. Board* was implemented.

Denise knows her history. She explains that the twenty years following Brown were characterized by white flight, or the exodus of white middle- and upper-class families from the cities to the suburbs. White families fled to avoid proximity to new Black neighbors, taking their economic, social, and cultural capital with them as well as their power to hold schools accountable. Denise paints the picture:

> There are private schools everywhere now. I always say that a private school is a public school that you pay for because most minorities cannot afford those private schools. But privates only teach regular education. They're not [necessarily] more advanced. It's "resegregation" because you have a lot of schools in the extreme suburban [communities] that are *all* white. The inner city, which was once all white is all Black now because all the whites moved out.

These early and new perspectives shaped Denise's approach as a single mother of two Black girls, Nicole and Christina, both of whom were academically gifted. Denise's number one priority became to ensure that her daughters did not experience the same types of disheartening schooling that she did as a girl. She resolved to advocate for them whenever necessary, but that proved to be more frequent than she had imagined.

As Nicole, the eldest, entered fifth grade, Denise saw her daughter's agency dampen. Around the same age that Denise was forced to confront overt racial prejudice as a child, her daughter began to experience an updated, more subtle form of structural racism. Academic tracking, a commonplace sorting practice in schools nationwide, was meant to place students according to their abilities.

When Nicole was set to enter middle school, Denise was shocked to learn that her daughter was placed on the standard and remedial track rather than the honors track. Nicole had made the Honor Roll every year in elementary school and performed extremely well on her standardized tests. Her intellect was esteemed by her teachers as well. These are the standard factors that typically decide students' middle school placements by the end of fifth grade. Being new to the district's school system, or the "township" schools as they were called, Denise did not question this placement, but she had no choice when the same thing happened to Christina a year later.

Denise began by voicing her concerns to Christina's fifth grade teacher, who happened to be the first African American teacher hired at that school back in the 1970s. Christina's teacher also could not understand why Christina was not placed in any honors-level classes. The teacher began to advocate for Christina, writing letters to the middle school, talking to some of the middle school teachers, and giving her special assignments to demonstrate her academic giftedness. Yet nothing budged the middle school.

Meanwhile, Denise did more research on the honors track. She learned about the classes offered, the curriculum, and the student–teacher ratios. The honors program served as a direct pathway to quality higher education options. Denise also learned that the honors program overwhelmingly served white students. Denise says,

> They were mostly all white students [in honors]. I mean to the level of 90-plus percent white. So you have a class of thirty-five students and maybe one, maybe two, were minority students. And [yet] the school district that we're in is majority-minority. Sixty-five to 75% of all students are minorities. Why are we in a majority-minority school system and the honors classes are essentially reserved for all white students?

The honors classes appeared to essentially be reserved for white students despite their minority status across schools.

Denise realized that her advocacy work was put to the test further when Nicole's sixth grade math teacher explained to Denise that on the basis of her observations that first month, Nicole was not ready for the honors track. The reason: Nicole lacked the necessary critical thinking skills. Denise knew that her daughter's grades, As and high Bs, contradicted this. Denise responded to the teacher,

> Well, don't you think kids should be challenged *more*? [Nicole] may struggle, but it serves to challenge her. Maybe she's not [demonstrating] her critical thinking or performing because she is not being *challenged* enough. You have to kind of know the kid. My daughter's a little bit lazy but she gets things very quickly. But if *you* stop there, *she's* going to stop there.

The math teacher was unconvinced, saying, "Maybe for next semester. We'll think about it." This was soon followed by a perplexing request from the same math teacher a year later for Denise's youngest daughter Christina to tutor an honors student. Denise and her daughter were baffled. "They look up to you enough for you to help the students who don't know the work," Denise recalls telling Christina. "But they won't let you be in the class."

Denise made phone calls to the middle school and the superintendent to learn more, eventually reaching the township's math coordinator in the Superintendent's Office. This person arranged for Christina to do *extra* assignments over the summer, which were then evaluated. On that basis, Christina was moved to the honors math track for seventh grade. In due course, Nicole was also moved into multiple honors courses in eighth grade, an outcome Denise credits to a new guidance counselor who had become aware of and involved in the girls' situation.

Getting in honors courses was one challenge, but navigating them was another. Although they wanted to be in honors classes, Denise's daughters began to feel that their mother's advocacy work made them negatively stand out, in a racially unfriendly environment. They began to resent their school, which became Denise's greatest "heartbreak":

> Once they were able to get into one or two of the honors classes, they felt isolated... They felt out of place as the only minorities in a lot of these classes. While they continued to perform, their attitude about schools started to get very negative. They felt a lot of pressure. My youngest started saying, "You know, Mom, it's like they don't think I know the work. I know all the answers, and it's still like I don't."

In honors courses, Nicole and Christina endured condescension from their teachers and white peers. At the same time, students, including friends in their regular classes, jeered at the girls for trying to "be white." Consequently, and naturally, this stigma surrounding honors classes kept Nicole and Christina from wanting to be in them. They also noticed the many resources their white peers had that many Black students didn't (e.g., involved parents, private tutors, international trips), which further lowered their self-esteem. Further, Denise says, the girls' teachers did not boost her daughters' self-confidence. Instead, many displayed "shock" at how involved Denise was in her daughters' education.

Denise's advocacy has thus expanded to getting her daughters to enjoy school again. Today, Chrsitina has graduated high school with an impressive record of achievement, including success in multiple AP courses. She received many college scholarship offers and is attending the same university where Nicole is enrolled. She has been directly admitted to a top-ranked business school following completion of her undergraduate degree.

Denise plans to continue to educate parents, especially those from underserved and underrepresented groups, by telling her story. These parents, Denise says, need to know about the "real" education system.

Chapter Summary

The storytellers in this chapter encourage us to lean in to our values, hunches, and beliefs. When opposing forces push us away from what matters to us we must exercise courage to persist and strengthen our sense of self. The two themes resonating across these stories concern how to maintain unwavering conviction and mobilize it to achieve equitable outcomes.

Equity-Oriented Leaders Stay Open to Divergent Thinking

Leaders who dare to promote equity in the face of staunch opposition routinely question existing systems—challenging norms that are usually taken for granted by others—including their own strongly held beliefs. Diane Ravitch's story exemplifies this type of critical reflection; over decades, she changed and revised fundamental opinions and approaches that had previously defined her career. Even the most veteran education professionals can be deluded into the perception that meritocracy and competition are the norm in US education. It takes divergent thinking to question whether these ideals are being realized and why the students who are more advantaged and privileged and thus have access to the best resources outperform others.[9]

As troubling information surfaced on the implementation of new policies Diane had endorsed, including No Child Left Behind (NCLB), Diane publicly questioned her former assumptions, unlike other leaders. NCLB data demonstrated that race- and class-based disparities continued despite NCLB's claim of accountability. NCLB penalized failing and underfunded schools through high-stakes testing and standards that ignored local contexts.[10] Ravitch, directly opposing her professional networks and colleagues, bravely and openly disavowed these mandates. She let go of knowledge that no longer made sense, shedding a type of cultural capital.

But her pivot meant forgoing powerful professional networks and personal relationships—a lifetime's worth of social capital. Ravitch endured the ostracization because she cared more about education than maintaining flawed views. While this book highlights the benefits of networks, Ravitch's story illustrates that leaders must also sometimes forfeit social capital if it frustrates their aims.

Pedro Noguera also shows us that when expectations, hypotheses, and values are not met, great leadership steps out of comfort zones

---

[9] Anthony P. Carnevale, Peter Schmidt, and Jeff Strohl, *The Merit Myth: How Our Colleges Favor the Rich and Divide America* (New Press, 2020); Stephen J. McNamee and Robert K. Miller Jr., *The Meritocracy Myth*, 2nd ed. (Rowman & Littlefield, 2009); Jonathan Kozol, *Savage Inequalities: Children in America's Schools* (Crown, 2012).

[10] Diane Ravitch, "Time to Kill 'No Child Left Behind,'" *Education Digest: Essential Readings Condensed for Quick Review* 75, no. 1 (2009): 4–6; D. Hursh, "Exacerbating Inequality: The Failed Promise of the No Child Left Behind Act," *Race Ethnicity and Education* 10, no. 3 (2007): 295–308.

and changes. Typically, we do not associate a resignation with an opportunity to incite progress. Noguera's resignation, however, exposed hypocrisies within the system he had been operating in. This act required humility as well as courage. Those who carry the most political power and decision-making influence, such as the state politicians in Noguera's story, are often unwilling to hear challenges to their agendas. Noguera teaches us that while unequal power dynamics always exist within any institution or hierarchy, they do not have to be debilitating. The best educational leaders constantly question premises; they build power where they can despite systemic and institutional barriers.

Our other storytellers also forged new paths with their unwavering activism and advocacy. Shani Robinson, with years of effort, restored her reputation, another form of deeply personal cultural capital. Olivia Mok reignited her identity and voice as an Asian American to reconfirm her place and belonging within the AANHPI community. Denise Williamson advocated for her daughters when she realized they were experiencing a new, modern form of racism in school, one that was similar but different from the racism she endured during the era of school desegregation. These stories show us that when others are dead set on following an unjust path, resistance itself becomes cultural capital that must be built and disseminated.

Leaders Secure Allyship by Leveraging Communication

No leader should have to go it alone—that trope stalls progressive change. But disrupting the status quo can be an isolating experience. Educational leaders often have to get creative in disseminating their message to audiences to garner support.

To maintain existing relationships, Noguera was transparent with his allies, stakeholders, and the public about his reasons for resigning from the charter authorizing committee. Many, including the staff at SUNY, strongly supported him because they understood the dynamics troubling him. The highest ranks, however, did not. Though Noguera could have quietly departed from his post, he leveraged the media to generate awareness of his cause. His familiarity with engaging in public discourse provided him access to the press, and that access in turn was a vehicle to disseminate his reasoning. The public learned that he resigned because of evidence he collected and that he was driven by equity-minded calculations and not emotions.

Leaders should consider all communication channels and creatively use them to spread their messages. Shani Robinson co-authored her book, *None of the Above*, with journalist Anna Simonton, to expose the ills of the existing educational and judicial systems. She turned her tribulations into a resource for others, offering the new forms of knowledge and cultural capital she had gained in support of educators who were marginalized by the system. Shani shed light on how Black educators, particularly those serving disinvested communities, often pay the price for a system that does not adequately support them. One of Robinson's messages was to advise other educators to seek mentors among veteran educators and discover grassroots organizations that can champion them. Having been isolated and having supporters turn their backs on her, Robinson spoke from direct experience on the necessity of building social capital. For Olivia, her advocacy work was bolstered by the ASAP community, who empowered her conviction and identity as an Asian American. From being a shy eighth-grader to now being an aspiring sociologist, Olivia continues to build more allies and mentor young AANHPI community members to promote awareness and conversations about social structures affecting our communities.

Denise Williamson sought support from those who could corroborate her daughters' qualifications, finding allies in the township's math coordinator at the Superintendent's Office and in a new guidance counselor. While others treated her concerns as unfounded, these professionals allowed her to realize she was justified in seeking to expand pathways to opportunity for her daughters. Maintaining steadfast conviction benefits from forging bonds with allies when others have turned their back. Without the help of others, it is often challenging to find the strength we need to keep ourselves going.

5

Hand-Ups Over Handouts
Promote Agency Above All Else

CHAPTER CO-AUTHORED WITH GABRIELLA PORTELA, DOCTORAL CANDIDATE, FLORIDA INTERNATIONAL UNIVERSITY, EDUCATIONAL LEADERSHIP

DESPITE GOVERNMENT COVID-19 FINANCIAL relief reducing the national child poverty level to a historically low 5.2%, the long-standing negative perception of these programs—including direct stimulus payments and Expanded Child Tax Credits (CTC)—led Congress in 2021 to vote against continuing to provide wraparound assistance to families.[1] The national child poverty level soon shot back up to pre-pandemic levels.[2] Ideological critics call this type of aid "handouts," fearing that welfare, charity, and social services can lead recipients to grow overly dependent on outside assistance as well as drain society economically. Even those who to some degree believe in handouts know that the relief they provide is generally temporary; giving a panhandler

---

[1] Danillo Trisi, "Government's Pandemic Response Turned a Would-Be Poverty Surge into a Historic Reduction in Poverty," Center on Budget and Policy Priorities, January 12, 2023, https://www.cbpp.org/research/poverty-and-inequality/governments-pandemic-response-turned-a-would-be-poverty-surge-into.

[2] Matthew Desmond, *Poverty, By America* (Crown, 2023).

loose change may help them in the short term, but it does nothing to address the systemic barriers such marginalized community members experience routinely. This is also typically the logic that underpins many criticisms of welfare programs.

These moral and political conversations often miss an important distinction: handouts are not the same as hand-*ups*. Hand-ups help people help themselves, providing life skills, education, and awareness of resources so individuals can problem solve and take control of their lives. The term has been part of the US vernacular since around the 1930s. Whereas a handout can be offered from afar and be without community ties, hand-ups tend to come from a person or group seeking to partner with a community in distress.

For example, the group New Jersey Veterans Stand Down not only gives donations to unhoused veterans but also educates them about available programs and provides services such as transportation to and from programming. This not only provides opportunities, but also lowers barriers so that those who are being helped can develop agency to thrive on their own.

The Atlanta-based community developer Robert Lupton, founder of Focused Community Strategies (FCS) Urban Ministries, believes hand-ups equip students in adverse circumstances with the tools, knowledge, and resources needed to overcome systemic challenges. FCS's most significant hand-up has been food co-ops and pantries that also teach culinary skills and the essentials of food production.

Programs promoting empowerment, community development, and self-sufficiency are not new. What is new is the educational community's willingness to embrace the hand-up philosophy. This acceptance is justified by the long-term benefits to students of hand-ups shown in research about positive psychology (ways to improve character strengths and self-reliance) and studies finding that hand-ups give students lifelong skills of active learning, and autonomy.

The late Brazilian educator Paulo Freire believed that education should be a means for students to critically engage with their reality and actively participate in transforming their circumstances. This transformation ideally results in agency, or as I define it, "a person's capacity to leverage resources to navigate obstacles and create positive change in their lives."[3] Although agency generally operates at an individual level, it has collective elements. There can also be social agency when collective groups work toward advancing a beneficial aim for all.

While a person's individual agency may advance their ability to overcome personal challenges (such as pursuing education in prison), structural changes and barrier reductions are still needed to make that education available. These changes require combined effort from educators, students, and the community. Educational and community leaders, in particular, should mentor students to chart their own courses, acting as GPS systems for students stuck in "learning traffic."[4]

The stories in this chapter—from Arne Duncan, Lisa Delpit, James Whitfield, Jacqueline Rodero, and Pete Kadens—portray agency for students as critical. They contrast the deficits of traditional, charitable handout thinking with the value of hand-ups, which address immediate challenges and instill self-sufficiency. Their programs inspire individuals to work through difficult situations and then help others create more equitable systems for all learners.

We Have to Look Out for Each Other: Crisis Requires Community
STORYTELLER: ARNE DUNCAN
Managing partner, Chicago CRED, and former US Secretary of Education

Conventional teaching and outreach methods are not always sufficient for disinvested communities and the students within them. Sometimes, the students who experience poverty, violence, neglect, and trauma (referred to by some as the "invisible backpacks" young people carry) require deeper forms of support and holistic opportunities to mitigate. Arne Duncan, former Secretary of Education under President Barack Obama, embraces such a perspective, one he gained early in life.

---

[3] Anindya Kundu, *The Power of Student Agency: Looking Beyond Grit to Close the Opportunity Gap* (Teachers College Press, 2020).
[4] Jacob Bruno, "How to Build Student Agency in Your Classroom," NWEA, July 15, 2021, https://www.nwea.org/blog/2021/how-to-build-student-agency-in-your-classroom/.

Born and raised in Chicago, Arne says, "Education was sort of our family business." Arne's father, Starkey, was a professor at the University of Chicago. His mother, Sue, took a less conventional route, recognizing that Chicago's inner-city children needed more than the traditional offerings of the classroom. In 1961, she established the Sue Duncan Children's Center in Chicago, a nonprofit program for inner city youth.

The Center offered free after-school and summer tutoring and other academic programs in addition to extracurricular activities. Arne and his two siblings spent much of their childhood working at the Center. "Mom literally raised all of us as a part of her program," Arne says with a touch of nostalgia. Her crusade left an indelible imprint on his heart.

In 1991, following a decorated career playing professional basketball in Europe, Arne and his sister established the Chicago chapter of I Have a Dream (IHAD). IHAD focused on offering low-income children and their families support echoing Sue Duncan's program, including meals, transportation to outside activities, and engagement with extended family members. IHAD encouraged parental involvement and provided adults resources to enhance stability in their home. Arne took an active part in every aspect of IHAD, including picking up kids from every corner of Chicago and transporting them to extracurricular activities. Arne was known as the "guy with the white van."

IHAD was a resounding success. "Our students graduated at an 89% graduation rate, but the class that started one year ahead of us, which didn't have the opportunities we provided, had a mere 33% graduation rate." Arne lingers on this thought. "Same kids, same community, same school building, just a one-year difference. We tried to prove that all kids can be successful when given opportunities and love and guidance and support." Arne was inspired to scale this work.

After serving as Secretary of Education from 2009 through 2015, he became managing partner of Create Real Economic Destiny (CRED) in 2016. CRED's goal is to reduce gun violence by supporting inner-city men, women, and children. CRED partners with community leaders and organizations to offer a comprehensive educational approach of outreach, life coaching, counseling, and job training. Arne believes that eliminating nonacademic barriers allows children to realize their potential. CRED strives to steer children clear of negative influences present in their community, engaging in consistent (and persistent) outreach by being directly involved in neighborhoods and in homes. Here, Arne finds himself in his element. This type of community work feels more natural to him than the world of educational administration and politics, where he has become more recognizable.

Arne recalls a reunion with many of the program's alumni, some who overcame tremendous odds. Lawanda, once vulnerable to gang violence, had CRED's unwavering support and connected with mentors who helped her escape her violent neighborhood. Sandra, who lost both parents to addiction, joined the program thanks to a neighbor's encouragement. She is now a teacher. Wanda, who experienced domestic violence at home and even joined a gang for a short time, now leads a significant technology effort in Chicago. Tiffany, who grew up in an underserved neighborhood, now focuses her efforts on community development in Baltimore.

Organizations like CRED celebrate and encourage the interconnection of communities and the support of neighbors, especially in times of crisis. This power of community is crucial. "If it taught us nothing else, I think [the pandemic] taught us how interdependent we are," Arne says. "How we need each other, that if I'm healthy and my neighbor's not, then none of us are healthy. We really have to look out for each other, and there's no place [where that's] truer than education. If my kids are getting a good education, but my neighbors' aren't, then we all suffer."

The holistic approach embraced by Arne Duncan involves more than focusing on the child. Educators and mentors must interact directly with the community and encourage it to discover and take advantage of outside resources. This approach emphasizes that people don't need just charity or hard resources like money; they benefit more from soft resources and learning how to locate them for themselves—encouraging children and their families to access these resources and reach inside themselves to uncover hidden potential results in transformative change.

We create educational success by moving beyond traditional thinking, pushing for change outside the classroom and within neighborhoods, and enhancing everyone's learning capabilities by tackling barriers. This is not just about education; it's about generating real opportunity pathways. We lay the foundation for lasting, positive change by fostering self-sufficiency and empowerment within the community.

Reducing and Removing Barriers to Make Way for Capable People
STORYTELLER: LISA DELPIT
Principle, Delpit Learning

Dr. Lisa Delpit, an esteemed teacher, researcher, and award-winning author in education, has drawn from her life experiences as she advocates for transformative education. Born in 1952 in Baton Rouge, Lisa's upbringing in a racially segregated environment influenced her understanding of racial dynamics and its influences on young people. Once, young Lisa and her mother went to shop at a department store, where her mother was denied the simple act of trying on a hat. This was a relatively ordinary event. Lisa's family remained resilient and even altruistic despite the pervasive racism they endured.

Lisa's father, Thomas Delpit, was a self-made entrepreneur without formal education. With just forty-six cents, he started the Chicken Shack, a community restaurant. He provided free lunches for neighborhood children, addressing food insecurity and empowering the community.

Lisa was seven when her father died of kidney failure. He could not get access to a dialysis machine, a stark reminder of racial disparities in healthcare. Lisa attended a pre-integration Catholic school where, she recalls, the Black nuns corrected her speech to conform to standard English, reflecting societal biases. One nun's admonition to "act your age, not your color" epitomized the internalized views in society concerning Black people. This and other experiences of systemic racism and her father's community service inspired Lisa to pursue a lifelong career in education, focusing on addressing inequities faced by Black youth.

Through her teaching and scholarship, Lisa has showcased how and why educators must adopt creative, identity-affirming approaches and challenge standardized educational norms, such as curricula that predominantly features Western history and literature while marginalizing other cultures. While attending Harvard Graduate School of Education to pursue her master's and doctoral degrees in curriculum, instruction, and research, Lisa came to understand the importance of students learning to write while in meaningful contexts. Her conviction is eloquently captured in her statement during an interview with Education

Week: "Teaching is like telling a story, but you have to look at people while you are telling the story, and you can't tell the same story to everyone." One-size-fits-all education and systems of accountability only perpetuate the existing order, in which low-income students of color are further marginalized. Instead, we must establish formal schooling that affirms, celebrates, and leverages individuality and culture to propel achievement.

Lisa has gone on to have a prolific writing career, including authoring the groundbreaking *"Multiplication Is for White People,"* in which she urges educators to break the systemic mold and encourage marginalized youth to find their voice through education. Her *Teaching When the World Is on Fire* collects inspirational stories of those who have deftly navigated the suffocating culture wars to teach critical issues.[5] Lisa advocates for culturally relevant pedagogy—offering tailored hand-ups for students from diverse backgrounds—from which educators and students can forge profound relationships and affirm each other's value.

Lisa has also dismantled structural barriers for underrepresented people. In the 1990s, during Lisa's tenure at Georgia State University (GSU), she led urban teacher preparation programs. Across the US, these programs were struggling to recruit prospective Black educators. Lisa knew that Black teacher-candidates from low-income backgrounds faced insurmountable barriers because of low scores on the Graduate Record Exam (GRE).

Lisa boldly proposed eliminating the GRE requirement from student applications, a radical proposition at the time. Lisa explained, "I knew the GRE requirement would eliminate most of the teachers we wanted to bring in, especially African American teachers." The proposal went through, possibly because the administration missed seeing the provision, and the proposal became policy. Lisa knew that this had worked to her advantage and that the program would now be under more scrutiny. Luckily for Lisa and program participants, her hunch was right. Fifteen teachers, most Black, with GRE scores close to zero,

---

[5] Lisa Delpit, *"Multiplication Is for White People": Raising Expectations for Other People's Children* (The New Press, 2012) and *Teaching When the World Is on Fire* (The New Press, 2019).

eagerly stepped into the program, which trained them to teach in the communities they knew well.

These students, once hindered by standardized tests, went on to excel in their teaching careers. By the time the GSU dean acknowledged that Lisa's proposal had worked, the program was well established and thriving. "He kind of shook his head and said, 'Okay, okay,' and let us [keep doing] it, which was, again, unheard of at the time," Lisa recalls.

"It wasn't just about eliminating a test requirement," Lisa says regarding her strategy. "It was about giving these educators a chance to shine and break free from the psychological pressure of 'stereotype threat' that had clouded their paths. Testing has *nothing* to do with getting uniquely qualified teachers," Lisa explains. Subjecting students to a culturally biased test, such as the GRE, is unfair. Not only do these individuals perform below their potential on these exams—largely due to stereotype threat, or the fear of confirming the social biases that exist about their groups—they also lose confidence in their abilities.[6]

Another example of Lisa's commitment to dismantle rote learning is the Early College Program she founded under the Alonzo A. Crim Center for Urban Education Excellence (CUEE) at GSU. This program is for high school students who are interested in pursuing a teaching career after obtaining their bachelor's degree at GSU early. Essentially, this program gives low-income students of color the option of attending college with all expenses paid and then pursuing a fulfilling career unencumbered by student debt. Lisa also established urban leadership programs for principals and school district office staff in Atlanta, emphasizing the importance of teaching through storytelling and tailoring pedagogical stories to meet children's specific and developing cultural identities.

Lisa has long been an exemplar substantiating the idea that we can create the world we want to see through education. Often, achieving such a vision requires subversive acts to break existing, rigid, and exclusive molds around what education and its delivery should look like. Challenging norms to promote equity and opportunity requires

---

[6] Claude M. Steele, "A Threat in the Air: How Stereotypes Shape Intellectual Identity and Performance," *American Psychologist* 52, no. 6 (1997): 613.

innovative thinking that questions systems and the reasons for them. In doing so, Lisa invites us to reimagine not just education, but the very foundations of a just society.

Jan's Dream: Create a Lasting Legacy by Fostering Belonging
STORYTELLER: JAMES WHITFIELD
Superintendent, Treetops School International

Jan Whitfield always wanted to be an educator. But between caring for her two sons and her husband (a Vietnam veteran who was often absent as well as severely addicted to drugs and alcohol), Jan had no time for herself. She worked at a K-Mart superstore in Midland, Texas, while holding down at least one or two other jobs simultaneously. Still, Jan's dream persisted. Eventually, Jan enrolled in a teacher preparation program at the University of Texas Permian Basin. She was diagnosed with leukemia shortly thereafter but continued studying for her degree.

When his mother got sick, James Whitfield was only a sophomore in high school, but he became the primary caretaker for his younger brother. Stressors mounted as Jan went into treatment and then lost her battle. Still, James received abundant love and care from his basketball coaches at school. They were the first Black men James saw in leadership positions, which left an indelible imprint on him. Additionally, James's group of friends shielded James from their illicit activities. His friends saw something in James and knew better than to ruin his future. "And so," James says, "there's a deep sense of purpose [behind] why I do what I do."

James pursued multiple degrees in education (bachelor's, master's, and eventually a doctorate), dreaming of becoming a basketball coach and providing student athletes the kind of support he received while growing up. To support himself while an undergraduate, he coached female athletes at an affluent high school in Keller, Texas, going against his initial desire to work with inner-city males. He learned that *all* students, regardless of their backgrounds, have "their own unique struggles." James recalls, "Even kids who are driving up [to school in a] Mercedes. There are still levels of trauma inflicted in their lives as well." James knew what the research has been showing us: that *all* students benefit from seeing Black males in school leadership positions.

After graduating college, James accepted a full-time position at a school with significantly less funding and more diversity. The students in his classes reminded him of his childhood and the feeling of being invisible. He paints a picture:

> You know, most of the teachers at the campus are vying for AP and advanced placement type [students]. I was like, "Give me the kids nobody else wants to teach. I want to teach [them]." They had the most severe behaviors. You also [had] the kids that could have taken advanced courses, but they didn't want to ... and nobody wanted to support them in that [endeavor]. [The system] wanted to level them down. This is a *systemic* problem.

Thus, even though his colleagues called going into administration "joining the Dark Side,"—a sentiment shared by many across education—James saw leadership as a chance to positively affect system-level change and help more students belong.

After earning his leadership credentials, James went to lead at a middle school "across the tracks" in Richland Hills. Compared to his other schools, this one was majority-minority with a student population of 85% students of color and one-third English language learners. James's peers seemed skeptical. "There were people I knew and respected in the district. They said, 'Congrats!' but also, 'Why do you want to go to *that* school?'" James says. He told them he knew that he could speak the language of the community and slowly help students avoid fulfilling the prophecy of negative people's low expectations. "They needed visibility," James says. "They needed someone that was going to be visible and someone that was going to make them feel visible. [The students] come to school with these invisible backpacks filled with all kinds of stuff before they enter the building."

James devised a plan. Every day, students would get three positive interactions with staff and educators as soon as they entered the building. One would be with him, and so, regardless of the weather, James welcomed students with music and a smile every morning.

Both educators and students thought that James's approach would not last. "He ain't gonna keep this up!" he heard them saying. But over time, James proved them wrong. "By the third week, I knew facial expressions. I knew body language. I saw them every morning." If a student looked off, James would pull them aside to offer a caring conversation. "We were able to offset a lot of [issues] and get kids straight to the counselors' offices," instead of heading to class, where they might be upset enough to cause disruptions.

James also made changes to the master schedule. He increased access to advanced courses and allowed these courses to accommodate more students, ensuring that students' diverse needs would be supported. Over time, staff at James's school started noticing changes in how other educators from other schools around the district addressed and listened to them. Whereas before, they'd have largely been ignored at professional development convenings, now people asked them for insights.

James was promoted early and often. In 2020, he became the principal of Heritage High School after only a short stint as an assistant principal, thus becoming the first Black male principal to serve the school. After the murder of George Floyd, James sent a personal email out to friends and colleagues. Like most, he had been shaken by the news. James offered himself to others as a resource to find reflection, solidarity, and healing. In the letter, he mentioned that "systemic racism is alive and well" and wondered what could be done about it.

In the immediate term, James's stakeholders, including parents and staff, thanked him for sending the message. But later that fall, as election cycles ramped up and political tensions rose across the state, educators began receiving extra scrutiny. "The school board elections became very contentious. You also started to see a lot of requests for open records from people in the community who, by the way, were not parents of students. They were community members requesting records on anything that said racism, equity, or diversity and inclusion. George Floyd was one of the key terms," James recalls.

One year later, the Texas governor, Greg Abbott, banned critical race theory in K-12 public school classrooms. At a school board meeting, James was accused, *by name*—which went against the procedural etiquette of such proceedings—of plotting to infuse critical race theory concepts at the school by a former, failed school board candidate. James denied these claims. However, the school board decided not to renew James's contract and instead to place him on paid administrative leave.

While many might have chosen to retreat, James has leaned into leadership. He has been writing and speaking out (to community groups, aspiring educators, and nonprofit organizations, and he even testified before Congress) about public education leadership and working for equity. James has also been coaching educators nationwide who have faced similar accusations and tensions in their posts. "I want to be about my purpose, and I'm going to be about my purpose," James says. "I would not have changed a single thing [that resulted as a consequence of my actions].... I stood firm. The lesson I've learned is that leadership matters." Undeterred and impassioned, James pushes onward. He is guided by the enduring dream of his mother, Jan Whitfield, who knew and understood the power of education to promote positive social change for those who needed it.

From Adversity to Advocacy: Mentorship for Lasting Change
STORYTELLER: JACQUELINE RODERO
Student, Florida International University

Jackie Rodero was thrust into the foster care system at the age of seventeen. She then moved between three different homes in a short time. Despite this turbulence, Jackie found a consistent source of support from her education. "Ever since I was a little girl, I found my strength in school," Jackie says.

School was not simply a routine; it provided her a stable lifeline amidst an otherwise chaotic situation. In 2023, Jackie graduated from Coral Gables Senior High School with a rigorous international baccalaureate degree. The advanced coursework not only challenged her but also gave promise of a brighter future. "I'll get *something* out of this," Jackie would tell herself as a form of encouragement and motivation.

Jackie's favorite person at school was "Ms. B," a guidance counselor who went above and beyond as a mentor. "She was like a second mom [to me]," Jackie says. Throughout Jackie's teenage years, Ms. B offered

Jackie emotional support and helped her meet her basic nonacademic needs, from food to safety. Jackie was walking six miles daily to and from school from her foster home, which was past the end of the metro line and not served by any bus routes. Once her assigned court judge for foster care, Judge Bernstein, became aware of her situation, she was moved to a foster home closer to her school. Different people, from Jackie's judge to her principal, to the school's resource officer, and her teachers helped Jackie maintain a positive outlook. "I could always rely on my teachers. If I needed to send an email to get clarification on an assignment or lecture, they would sit down with me during and after school to explain concepts and what I missed... They would also make sure to check up on me," Jackie recalls.

Jackie's experience is certainly a rare one amongst the hundreds of thousands of US foster children. "I don't see [cases like mine] often in the foster care system, where foster youth [also] get the support they need through their school system," she says, speaking from direct knowledge. Today, as a Golden Scholar at Florida International University, Jackie is majoring in criminal justice, where she has the opportunity to observe foster care court proceedings at the Unified Children's Court. Through the Golden Scholars program, her college education is fully funded through Pell grants and scholarships.

One of the UCC judges, Judge Caballero, became so impressed with Jackie that she asked Jackie to come regularly to witness her court's proceedings, and to offer her mentorship for her career pathway. In this opportunity, Jackie was soon appointed as the inaugural director of peer advocacy. In this formal mentor role, Jackie provides foster children with necessary resources they are missing—the kind of support she received from professionals like Ms. B.

Jackie tailors her approach to meet the specific needs and challenges of the young people she supports. Many of her peer mentees have never been to school. Jackie's approach centers on guiding these youth to stay motivated and resilient, avoid the streets, and eventually pursue college. She guides them primarily by offering constant connection, offering many of them daily support through phone calls. Jackie, still a teenager herself, works hard to be a comforting presence to her mentees, who look up to her example.

She teaches them to read and write and gradually introduces new concepts so her mentees do not get overwhelmed. After all, Jackie knows better than most how these young people's lives are often overwhelming. "I want to increase their resilience and endurance through tiny steps," she says. Jackie strives to "be there" for her mentees, as both a dependable mentor and a friend, to ensure they never feel alone. They need to know someone is in their corner, and more often than not, that person is Jackie.

As peer director, Jackie works with two teenagers and four children but says that she is open to working with as many students as possible, despite all else she has on her plate as a college sophomore. She knows she can form connections with teenagers that others cannot. The foster care system is not necessarily built for managing the needs of teens, Jackie says. Jackie plans to become a judge in the UCC and, in that role, hopes to change this current structure of the foster care system one day. "You'll see this all the time, where [teens] just want someone to motivate them and say, 'Hey, I know what you're going through. I've been there. Let me show you the other side.'"

Jackie's story is a testament to the transformative power of education *and* mentorship. During Jackie's senior year, Ms. B suggested Jackie put her talents and ambitions toward pursuing a career in law, where Jackie could make a difference. Jackie's subsequent journey, as a high schooler navigating the foster care system to a peer leader advocating for systemic change, highlights the effect that holistic support can have on a young person's life. "I learned that I have to pay it forward," Jackie says, "so that someone else can see [there is] good in the world." Through her efforts, Jackie not only improves the lives of young people directly but inspires a broader movement toward systemic reform.

Tailored Resources Are the Seeds That Spark Community Empowerment
STORYTELLER: PETE KADENS
Chairman of the Kadens Family Foundation

Pete Kadens carries with him a deeply ingrained perspective on poverty, shaped by experiences both at home and around the globe. When he was eight years old, Pete's father received an academic sabbatical from the University of Toledo. Pete's family took this opportunity to travel expansively, venturing to twenty different countries. These early travels left a lasting effect on Pete, exposing him to many cultures and landscapes. What stood out to Pete were the stark realities of socioeconomic disadvantage and abject poverty across the globe. Pete also got a glimpse of geopolitical history, from China's rising communist regime to the then-flailing USSR's most remote and destitute regions.

"It was a fascinating experience for a young boy whose aperture was very much a middle-class, pretty easy lifestyle in middle America." Pete says. "When I saw other kids my age suffering the way they were suffering, the aperture opened up to [include] poverty and all of its different permutations." This anthropological journey of sorts set a foundation for Pete's belief in providing opportunities over simply offering charity to those in need.

Upon returning to Toledo, Pete's expanded perspective took in the more subtle forms of peril faced by others in his community. Going against his peers' misconceptions about the kids from the neighboring Scott High School—many of whom were poor Black students living in disinvested communities—Pete saw potential. For instance, in many of these extremely low-income homes, the family livelihood depended on the cultivation of cannabis in basements and garages. These operations required a level of skill and entrepreneurship which was reflected in the young people who grew up around them. Pete also knew of a student who, even though they had their college education fully funded by the HOPE program, deeply considered dropping out because they needed an extra $500 a month for food and medical bills. Pete understood the gravity of weighing these decisions and opportunity costs, which threatened to derail years of hard work. He became determined to not simply provide access to opportunities, but to also lower barriers.

Pete explains, "The truth is that I won [in my privileged position] because they lost [out on privilege]. And if I ever got really wealthy, I knew I wanted to pay it backward." It's a principle he lives by, always seeking to give back to those who may have suffered or struggled in order for Pete to succeed. True to his word, after financial success with his cannabis company (the second largest of its kind in the world), Pete retired in 2018, motivated to give back. He began by taking a teaching position at Johnson College Prep, a public charter school in Chicago's Englewood, a low-income neighborhood with many foreclosed homes and high crime rate.

Pete knew that simply teaching at the school was not enough. After seeing firsthand the potential of his students and the financial obstacles many faced, he also established the Kadens Family Foundation, implementing a scholarship program that covered not only tuition but also all other conceivable expenses that could hinder a student's success. The goal was to level the playing field and go beyond offering only temporary forms of relief. Pete's goal was for all students to pursue their education without financial strain.

Pete wants to ensure that all students have a shot at obtaining a college degree. "What I learned at college was the freedom to think," Pete recalls. "I was given [a chance] to conceptualize my life and define it [on my own terms]—not by the parameters that my parents or my family or anyone else set forth for me. I was given the ability to hear different perspectives and decide for myself how I wanted to interpret those perspectives." By providing to less-privileged students, through his teachings in business and entrepreneurship, this same opportunity to gain important skills and engage in deep reflection, Pete believes he is playing a small part in ushering in the next great generation of innovators. He empowers students with practical skills and fosters their entrepreneurial spirit, aiming to inspire them to emerge as future leaders and innovators in their respective fields.

After teaching and establishing his scholarship program for students in Chicago, Pete decided to return to the community he grew up in, Toledo, to pay it forward. During a scholarship ceremony in Toledo, Pete implored the audience of graduates to see his contributions not as gifts but as *responsibilities*. The crowd roared in agreement, seeing the scholarships were an investment in their community. In one touching case, the Foundation sponsored a young man's college education and funded his mother to accompany him and act as his sign language interpreter. Sometimes providing an opportunity is not enough; barriers must also be lowered for the opportunity to be seized.

The Kadens Family Foundation addresses young people's immediate needs but also looks after their future. The foundation aims to create an ecosystem where students are seen, not simply as beneficiaries, but as contributors to society. The goal is empowerment. "Investing in someone," Pete notes, "goes beyond the dollars. Believing in them can give them the self-esteem and confidence they need to succeed." Atypically for philanthropic organizations, the Kadens Family Foundation promotes creating environments where students can thrive on their own terms and by their own merits, providing a ladder but also helping to develop the skills to climb it. These efforts reshape how communities engage with and uplift their emerging leaders, ensuring that the support they receive is meaningful, transformative, and generated from within.

Chapter Summary

While *handouts* may offer temporary relief to those who receive them, they rarely address the root causes of structural phenomena, such as intergenerational poverty, deep traumas, or societal neglect. As such, handouts can perpetuate a cycle of diminished agency. In contrast, hand-*ups* can build long-term resilience and independence, equipping individuals with the skills, knowledge, and resources necessary to navigate difficulties as well as allowing receivers to develop purpose and contribute back to their communities. Here are the main lessons from this chapter.

Reduce Barriers Through Education and Tailored Resources to Promote Agency

Students can transform circumstances when they develop critical thinking through their educational experience. The path to unlocking their agency begins with honest assessments of students' burdens and barriers. From the initial inventory, educators, students, and community members can unite over shared goals to overcome obstacles. Only by tuning in to the particular needs of each student can educational leaders provide students with the tools needed to retake the helms of their lives. When young people get stuck, adults and peers can serve to remind them—through positive reinforcement—that there are social supports meant for navigating life's multifaceted obstacles. No one should have to go it alone.

Arne Duncan made it his mission to address root causes of academic disengagement though Chicago CRED. The significant gaps in achievement he noticed weren't due to inadequacy, but community and structural challenges including the gun violence sweeping across South Side communities. Duncan's CRED team partnered with local leaders and organizations to bring students and their parents practical help, such as outreach programs, one-on-one coaching, counseling, and job training. CRED helps students identify and overcome interpersonal, institutional, and systemic obstacles, giving them a sense of control and direction.

Jackie Rodero's story demonstrates that receiving such targeted support can be a lifeline for marginalized communities. As an undergraduate student, Jackie pinpointed a glaring need in foster youth support: a sense of community to provide stability during a turbulent and formative time. Her solution? A peer mentor group connecting those with similar struggles and victories. With empathy, Rodero skillfully redirects mentees from street struggles toward higher education, acting as an example of the futures that can be constructed when a community embraces you.

Hindrances may still remain. Success does not come from providing one or two resources but from wraparound support which creates safe zones. When Lisa Delpit removed the GRE program, she created a whole lane for students to run through in order to thrive.

Community-Based Bonds Are Key to Developing Authentic Social Welfare

Close-knit community-based alliances among schools, students, and local partners are often effective against systemic barriers. Those most impacted by particular forms of societal neglect—those closest to the problems—must be invited to participate in solutions-building. Without these voices, change is not authentic and thus unsustainable.

Pete Kadens is an inspiring example of authentic coalition building. Kadens's outside-the-box approach created a high-impact and sustainable scholarship program. Of course, the financial aid from the foundation matters immensely, but the comprehensive support the foundation offers, beyond tuition, helps students find stability and a safety net held up by community members.

Through her work at the Crim Center for Urban Education Excellence, Lisa Delpit removed a significant barrier preventing low-income students of color from entering the teaching profession. With Delpit's and other educators' guidance, a dynamic group of students evolved into dedicated educators, anchoring themselves firmly in the neighborhoods they knew, paying forward the investment made in them. Educated individuals prepare educated individuals and the community investments compound. Through contagious confidence, people uplifted by the system are often inspired to pay it forward, creating a chain reaction of goodwill and change.

Achieving fairness across education depends on collective effort. Imagine a school, workplace, or community where everyone feels valued, needed, and supported—in such environments, collaboration fuels the engine. With a razor-sharp focus on a community's unique energy and positive attributes, programs like Kadens's and Delpit's can seed enduring equitable progress.

Social welfare initiatives succeed or fail on the strength of community bonds. The initiatives by Delpit, Duncan, Kadens, Rodero, and Whitfield were instrumental in reshaping whole systems to give everyone a more equal shot at being validated and valued.

Promoting Belonging Is Key to Empowering Others

James Whitfield knew his students carried invisible backpacks; he eased the weight on their shoulders by strengthening their self-esteem and fostering a culture of warm support and high expectations. As staff banded together to greet students each day, the students felt seen. In this way, Whitfield went beyond focusing on academic achievement, prioritizing student empowerment. Also, he opened doors to college prep courses and robust extracurricular activities which his students had not been offered. But once offered, the students lived up to the challenge of excelling in them. Other leaders in his district began to take notice.

Similarly, Delpit, Duncan, Rodero, and Kadens uplifted constituents by fostering sense of belonging. Students came to believe that they mattered when their dignity was upheld. (This is the central concept of Chapter 6.) People are capable of more than we often give credit for. Hand-ups that recognize the inherent potential in each individual create conditions that breed resilience, altruism, and solidarity.

6

Center Human Dignity

Champion All People's Right to Receive a Transformative Education

WHAT DRAWS PEOPLE TO WORK in education? Overwhelmingly, the majority of professionals across educational fields report that they are motivated by the desire to make a positive difference in their communities.[1] In addition to being drawn to this vocational calling, individuals who are passionate about improving the lives of others (through education) have a heightened sense of *belief* in other people. After all, if educational professionals did not fundamentally believe everyone to be capable of astonishing feats, then their efforts would seemingly be for naught. As the preceding chapters have reviewed, many existing programs, techniques, and practices have overcome roadblocks to equity.

Chapter 6 is about how we can mobilize these sentiments toward action and progressive change, through centering human dignity. Our

---

[1] School of Education, "5 Reasons the Best Educators Became Teachers," American University, 2018, https://soeonline.american.edu/blog/5-reasons-the-best-educators-became-teachers/#:~:text=According%20to%20a%20recent%20survey,they%20enjoyed%20working%20with%20children.

storytellers exemplify how to harness a belief in others and apply this championship to improve unjust systems. We will learn how to best represent the perspectives and challenges of others through leadership, and how putting others first allows us to be brave in the face of powerful oppositional forces. Ultimately, the leaders of Chapter 6 showcase that acts of service allow us to be our best selves, while bringing out the best in other people—even if neglected, deprived, and unsupported.

Education as a public good and universal right is a bipartisan view. Despite today's volatile climate surrounding education, historically, the basic idea that every child deserves a quality public education has cut across party lines. Perhaps the ongoing attacks on our educational systems and upon academic freedom are part of a calculated attempt to spread divisiveness.

In order to protect and improve public education, we must come together to uplift it as our greatest collective responsibility. Fighting back against the special interests tearing education apart requires collective agency and alignment of values. Though we may differ on which specific policies and approaches are best for improving school systems to support more stakeholders, we should be able to agree that a major goal of education is upholding the dignity of those receiving it. The following stories show us how.

Testifying for Good: Applying One's Influence to Give Greater Platform to Others
STORYTELLER: MICHELLE FINE
Distinguished professor at the City University of New York

Throughout her career, Michelle Fine has felt compelled to move beyond simply studying social problems. She addresses root causes in and around education and criminal justice. To better understand how race, class, and gender-based inequalities compound and affect people, Michelle uses interdisciplinary traditions from fields like American studies, urban education, and critical, social, and environmental psychology. Michelle draws on her family history to explain her interdisciplinary approach to examining every side of a problem:

> I am the child of immigrants, refugees, Jews who came here in the early twenties as children. The wisdom of immigrants and immigrant children is that we know there are many ways to tell the story of what could be otherwise and what's natural. There's wisdom that grows at the margins. White privilege gave us a little fracture into which my father, who sold plumbing supplies and was in World War II, could enter. I grew up with bifocals on, on [the] one hand knowing marginalization, and on the other hand, having the sense that white skin was getting us into stuff, which you and I might now call assimilation.

For Michelle it has been impossible to separate the idea of work from identity and heritage. She credits her unique "bifocal" vantage as motivating her to engage in critical yet approachable work, which is demonstrated through her humanistic writing, deft storytelling, and attention to students' lived realities. Michelle has also participated as an expert witness in more than a dozen high-profile education lawsuits challenging the systematic exclusion of students from quality education throughout the K-16 pipeline.

Typically, Michelle testifies in cases that involve "low-income youth of color [who get] inadequate facilities, books, expectations, and stable relationships with educators," she says. In 2022, Michelle served as an expert witness for the Baltimore chapter of the National Association for the Advancement of Colored People (NAACP), in a lawsuit it brought for low-income Black children who were getting insufficient state funding. Michelle testified about the daily social and psychological impacts that diminished resources have on kids, drawing from decades of experience and research.

Michelle did not always see herself getting involved with this kind of work. Her first request to be an expert witness came when she was teaching at the University of Pennsylvania in 1982. The case, *Newberg v. Board of Public Ed*, involved one of the best Philadelphia high schools, which admitted only male students at the time. A group of girls and their families sued to get access. Michelle provided testimony on why public institutions for young men should be open to young women and how this disproportionate access and gender disparity affects life outcomes. Then, in the early 1990s, Michelle testified in a case in Wedowee,

Alabama where a principal canceled the Prom because of biracial dating within the school. "But this could've happened tomorrow," she says, when recounting the story. Soon after that, she received a request to testify in a lawsuit against the Citadel in South Carolina, a military academy that unknowingly admitted a female who left gender blank on her application. When the academy found out she was a woman, it refused her admission.

As requests kept coming, Michelle found many intrinsic rewards in her participation, one of which was meeting and connecting extraordinary people. She says:

> I meet bold educators who wish [the system] was different. Part of the joy of being an academic is that I can help folks find each other, like brave principals in Miami who dared to say, "We're going to protect our children and their families. We're going to protect our teachers with vaccines, masks, et cetera," despite what the state said. COVID taught us that educational leaders do God's work. But they need to be linked to each other, because it's lonely and hard.

Still, Michelle admits, participating in high-stakes work can lead to undesired consequences out of her control. She has since rethought her position in the Citadel case that argued for allowing young women into the military. During her deposition, the Citadel's lawyer had asked Michelle if she was afraid women admitted into the program could get raped. At the time, Michelle thought this was simply an argument for exclusion, but looking back, she admits she may have been shortsighted:

> I'm not sure getting young women into that institution was a way to build toward a more just, pacifist future. Now young women at war are often sexually abused by peers and don't have protections. Nothing changed. They added female bodies into what's often, not always, a kind of white supremacist, misogynist, homophobic culture. People of color and/or women, or people who are gay or gender expansive, pay a huge price because nothing else shifted. You can't just move bodies into institutions.

Though Michelle had testified in accordance with her values then, today she realizes she may have been naive and without the complete picture.

The underlying structures—such as the male-dominated, misogynistic culture of the army—are what give organizations rigid shape and are hard to challenge without implementing sweeping structural change in addition to more inclusive policy.

After the 2008 economic downturn, Michelle testified in California for schools that were "hemorrhaging educators." Low-income schools issued most of the pink slips. Michelle took the side that if teachers had to get laid off *at all*, they should be laid off equitably, across the system. Michelle thus supported a flat layoff structure in which schools could not lose more than a certain percentage of their educators before pink slips were given out to other schools. But the next day, the *New York Post* printed an article, with a big picture of New York Mayor Bloomberg and Los Angeles Mayor Villaraigosa shaking hands, titled "First Nail in the Coffin of Tenure." Ending teacher tenure—a protection public educators rely on—had been these politicians' agendas. Michelle believes she had unknowingly become a pawn to their politics and their war on teacher's unions.

Today, Michelle is more intentional about cases she takes on, weighing their potential implications and unintended consequences. To keep her insights sharp, she maintains an active research agenda which is unique for a tenured and decorated distinguished professor. Her team recently presented data to the State of New York on Performance Standards Consortium, an alternative to high-stakes testing. Instead of standardized state-level tests, students engage in serious inquiry, where they perform thoughtful research across important subject areas and present projects to panels of peers and experts. From the culminating feedback, students strengthen their work. Their findings indicate that these students, especially men of color, are likelier to persist in college and have higher GPAs.

When asked what keeps her going, Michelle says:

> If you think there's an injustice, you're not the only one. You might be the only one to say it out loud. And my experience is, you can't just do the critique. You have to have an imagination for how things might be otherwise. I could rant about high-stakes tests, but we need to show this performance-based alternative framework. Even around school safety, everybody wants to be safe. That doesn't mean that we

need more police in schools or armed teachers, but we have to attend to the fact that people want to feel safe.

Throughout the pandemic, Michelle and her graduate students collected data from food service workers, bus drivers and other essential workers, students, parents, teachers, and principals, to learn about how public institutions and their workers were degraded. All over the country, disinvestments in public services affect vulnerable people who are deprived of the most basic resources. Aware of her unique position and privilege, Michelle says she wishes she did not need to do this kind of advocacy work, adding:

> There's something about my whiteness, my "academicness," my history, that makes it more or differently credible to juries, to judges. [We] shouldn't have to interview 150 people in Baltimore to say, "Come to the school with me. Look at the hole in the ceiling, look at the cockroaches in the water. Look at the old textbooks ... Would your children go to this school? Would you send someone you love here?" That should be a class trip rather than [my] expert testimony ... any Black seventeen-year-old could tell you this with a lot more fire from their belly.

Ultimately, Michelle Fine continues to do what any good educational leader does: she understands her position of power and influence and does not shy from it—she leans into it in order to try and incite the changes she wishes to see in the system.

For the Love of Books: Promoting Literacy (and Lifelong Education) as a Human Right
STORYTELLER: DEBRA BAZILE
Educator, Miami, Florida

For as long as she can remember, Debra Bazile has been a bibliophile. Debra's father, Mauratus, strongly influenced Debra's love of reading, but not because he was an avid reader himself. "He was born in Port-au-Prince, Haiti," Debra says. "When he was a young boy, he was the oldest son so he had to go to work. He didn't get to go to school ...

I didn't discover until I was seven years old that my dad couldn't read." Whenever she gave him handmade cards for his birthday and other holidays, Mauratus would flip them open and thank her, but Debra intuited that he didn't know what the cards said.

Debra still tells Mauratus, "I can teach you how to read, dad." But picking up literacy can be challenging at any age, let alone adulthood. "And even though he never became fully literate, he was so great at many other things," Debra says, proudly. "To this day, he doesn't store anyone's phone number in his phone and remembers them by heart." With Debra's encouragement, Mauratus enrolled in classes for English language learners at Miami-Dade Community College and then passed his US citizenship exam.

Because of his educational struggles, Mauratus insisted that Debra and her siblings take their education seriously. Debra took heed and became an excellent student, excelling throughout her K-12 education, college, and into graduate school. During her master's program at Florida International University (FIU), Debra took a children's literature course that played a major role in her life:

> Our [professor] used to read us children's books every single day. One day, she read us a story about a little girl [who] went to her friend's house and the friend read to her *Little Red Riding Hood*. The main girl thinks to herself, "That's not how my dad reads it to me. That's not how the story goes." She goes home and tells her dad that he's been reading the story wrong and discovers that her dad doesn't know how to read. Because he was uneducated. That day the levee broke for me.

Debra was overwhelmed by emotion. She was transported twenty years back in time, to when she was a girl full of sorrow that her father could not read.

Then she thought about her current profession—a kindergarten teacher to many immigrant children in Miami, Florida, a city of newcomers where her father also charted a new life. Many of Debra's students' parents did not speak English and thus, many likely could not read English either. Like Mauratus, these parents never had an opportunity for education, and they too had high hopes for their children. Debra resolved then and there that she would do everything in her power to help her students *and* their parents learn to read.

Debra told the parents of her students she would tutor anyone who wanted it. That year, eight parents started learning reading fundamentals from Debra.

Around the same time, Debra began to expand her classroom library at the encouragement of her professor. She brought books that had Spanish or Creole mixed in. "The kids went wild," she recalls. She visited a local library and asked if they had any children's books they were going to throw out. She received dozens more for her class. She encouraged students to meet her at the library and helped them get library cards. Parents came too. She organized story nights and helped students with homework.

She formed such a bond with her kindergarteners that year that she moved with them as they went on to first grade. She read to them every day, and their love for reading flourished. Her classroom reading area was magical, complete with a "tree" and comfortable chairs under it. "But then I started to notice that the books were missing, especially the ones [I had] recently read during story time . . . You know, with kindergarteners, you notice things. They can't really *hide* things. I would watch them casually pull books out, sometimes place them back, but sometimes hide them in their desk."

Whereas some would interpret this as students stealing, Debra did the opposite. Not for a second did she think of her students as deficient, but instead acknowledged the absence of opportunities in their lives. She realized a clear truth: these young children did not have books at home to call their own. They were not deficient in morals but deficient in opportunities.

Debra doubled down and expanded her network for book donations. Her vision was for her students to be able to hold books in their hands, carry them anywhere, and turn the pages anywhere that they roamed. In addition to her relationship with the library, Debra partnered with First Book Marketplace which donated $500 worth of books that first year to fill out her classroom library. She also created a Donors Choose project, Hungry for Sight Words, which gave students Dr. Seuss books, full of sight words, such as "the," "is," "of," and so on.

The following year Debra continued expanding access to books in schools. She secured additional funds for colleagues in her school to build out their classroom libraries. Only two teachers requested funding, so Debra distributed funds to elementary educators in other Miami-Dade public schools. In total, she supported five educators and their classroom libraries that year.

To this day, Debra shows no signs of slowing down. Every year, Debra has grown her network of partners and contributors, including a donation of $3,250 from a local business. When asked how she has built up such a robust network of charitable organizations, Debra says, "Just talking to people, networking, researching, and doing my due diligence—[for example,] emailing like a brand ambassador." By being an ambassador for literacy, Debra has grown her and other classroom libraries throughout Miami. In so doing, she helps children build their literacy on a foundation for their academic trajectories and future possibilities to grow from, as they secure brighter futures for not only themselves but their families and generations to come.

The Mother of All: The Only Option Is Love
STORYTELLER: JENNIFER BLANCHETTE
Lead teacher, Simon Youth Academy

The Simon Youth Academy (SYA) is a small alternative high school in Port Charlotte, Florida with a mission to help "at-risk" students earn their high school diploma after aging out of the traditional school system. The school, aptly called The Academy, is the only Dropout Prevention School in the area. Over half the student population is economically disadvantaged, and 37% of the students are Black and Latinx. Though alternative education is known to be pedagogically challenging, one teacher sees it as the only option to serve students with the most needs.

Jennifer Blanchette, a veteran teacher with thirty-one years of teaching experience, has quite a reputation in her community with her outstanding record as a teacher, parent, and leader. Her colleagues and relatives have come to know her as "the Mother of All," in recognition that she goes beyond the call of duty; she provides extra care and love for her students, going so far as to bring them into her home. When asked where this drive comes from to give her students the guidance and encouragement they need, Jennifer says she wants to support them—whether her students, biological children, or foster children—in the way she never was in her dysfunctional childhood.

Jennifer's disrupts the traditional, top-down student–teacher relationship by providing students with individualized attention and love:

> It's our passion to show children who need love that they *do* matter... That's something I always go back [to]. It doesn't matter how I feel or what's on my plate. This child needs this love and attention and to know that they matter more than anything else.

Jennifer's first principle is refusing to see her students as anything other than capable. This guiding value has led her to notice and cater to students' nonacademic needs first, as a foundation to relationship building. Jennifer's nurturing approach led two students to open up over time. Learning their lives outside of school were devoid of structure, safety, and familial support, she adopted these girls as her own. Jennifer knows she can't do that for all students, though if she had it her way, she'd adopt dozens more.

Professionally, what keeps Jennifer motivated and hopeful is the collaboration and camaraderie of her colleagues:

> At The Academy... many people there, who may not go to the extent that *I* do... have a passion for helping kids. They know outside of school is where most students' difficulties and adversities come from. I have a great network of colleagues that pick up the areas that I or others left off.

Jennifer knows that her students, many of whom have emotional and behavioral disorders, have trouble outside school, where there is less support. Instead of stigmatizing students as hopeless delinquents unready for the real world, Jennifer reminds her colleagues that they can pair students with specific resources that address their unique circumstances and lean on one another to help the student. "Find people within your tribe that can meet the [skills and abilities] that you may lack, because they're out there... there's always hope and there's always people trying to help."

Jennifer says it is equally important to influence the hearts and minds of community members at large. The SYA is in a community where a large number of residents are retired, and many of them view the students that the SYA serves as beyond rehabilitation. In 2022, a proposition to pour more financial resources into the schools was unpopular in the surrounding community because it would raise taxes. Jennifer and her colleagues went into the local areas to convince people to vote yes on the proposition. Jennifer's message to her neighbors was quite clear: if you are unwilling to support these young people, you are not allowed to complain about them. Her message that "investing in young people is investing in your own community's future" must have resonated. The proposition passed, even though similar ones had failed in previous years.

Obedience Will Only Get You So Far: Social Justice as an Insurgent and Imperative Approach
STORYTELLER: LISETTE NIEVES
President of Fund for the City of New York and distinguished clinical professor, New York University

Lisette Nieves is a proud Puerto Rican and Brooklynite. She says that to better understand her perspective on leadership for change, you need to start at the beginning. Thus, this story has components more akin to an origin story. Like a superhero.

Lisette's parents arrived in New York as small children in the late 1940s and 1950s as part of the largest air migration of migrants from Puerto Rico to the United States. When Lisette was four years old her birth mother died and for six months, Lisette and her sister were in foster care. Their father had to navigate the complexities of the foster system to get them out. "[Fortunately], they kept me and my sister together. The [foster] safety net worked. I'm not romanticizing it; I'm saying it worked for us, and I'm really grateful for that. It could have been horrific."

Lisette's childhood in 1970s New York was full of hypersegregation and white flight, in which thousands of white families moved out of the centers of Manhattan, Brooklyn, Queens, and the Bronx and settled in suburban neighborhoods like Staten Island, Scarsdale, and White Plains. They took with them much of the capital required for basic services. Lower-income families became more financially squeezed, were manipulated by unfair practices, and suffered from power being concentrated in the hands of a wealthy few. Lisette remembers that routine building maintenance inspections of her pre-war apartment building in Central Flatbush, Brooklyn, and other necessities that keep spaces safe were often neglected.

Despite these building hazards, Lisette's family and working-class neighbors—among them Black Americans and people from Latin America and parts of the Caribbean all worked and paid considerable rents. Lisette recalls,

> My parents joined other people in [our] building and started a rent strike. I'll never forget that. I was probably nine or ten years old. I would see them meeting monthly or more regularly than that. They met over a couple years. I saw what it was like for people to mobilize... The landlord of ours was a famous and well-known slum lord.... I would see them try to buy off my dad. People would come with a suitcase full of money to break a strike.

Over several years, the strikers remained impervious to pressures to yield. Finally, the landlord had no choice but to make required maintenance. "I [saw] up close, what does it mean for the working class and for the poor to stand up for themselves? What does it mean to stand up for dignity and rights?" Lisette says. She could have taken away a different lesson, however. In some respects, her life might have been easier if her father had accepted the payoff—especially because he was a working-class migrant from Puerto Rico fighting powerful and connected forces in the city. And Lisette learned another life lesson during these turbulent times. Her parents kept taking in family and friends into their home who needed help. These were folks combating health, addiction or finance issues. "I learned very early in my childhood that good people can make bad decisions that may have seriously unfair consequences," Lisette says.

Lisette entered young adulthood drawn to activism. At eighteen, she took a gap year before college and joined the City Volunteer Corps (a precursor to AmeriCorps). One of her assignments over the service year was working with people with AIDS. Lisette had family and close acquaintances who died from or living with AIDS infections. She was enraged and perplexed by the lack of public response to these tragedies, at a time when AIDS or HIV-positive diagnoses were death sentences.

"You're in the middle of this crisis." Lisette says, describing her motivation for the gap year. "You have a president who's not even saying that this is a crisis. You're seeing all these people dying around you. It's crazy. Now, there's a word for it, 'gaslit.' I was gaslit daily. I was like, 'Is it just me?" Lisette joined the Patient Relations Department of a public hospital that contained the first public-financed long-term AIDS ward in the US:

> I was signing all these living wills because people were just dying. Many were openly gay, almost all of color. I learned about drag and street culture. I was the young person who made sure they had the right red lipstick they wanted at the end [of their life]. I learned a lot. There's a lot of shades of red.

For Lisette, these experiences humanized and contextualized a sweeping epidemic that remained out of sight and out of mind for most of the general public. She took that with her to Brooklyn College, where she structured her honor's undergraduate coursework around understanding the impact of AIDS on impoverished and marginalized communities and how groups like churches enlisted in the fight, despite typically expressing different value systems. Lisette saw the connection between her studies as a political science and philosophy major and the outside world. She could link structural inequality to people's day-to-day lived experiences and felt an urgency to not wait for policy change. She also volunteered in Brooklyn for causes related to adult literacy and homelessness.

We continue to see traces of intergenerational traumas today, says Lisette. For instance, a low-income young person growing up in

Corona, Queens has likely experienced a family member passing away from COVID-19. Similarly, youngsters of the late 1980s who grew up in Washington Heights were affected by the devastation of the crack epidemic. To continue connecting structural inequality to people's day-to-day lived experiences, Lisette was awarded a Truman Scholarship to attend the London School of Economics, and later she became a Rhodes Scholar at the University of Oxford.

Lisette has gone onto hold senior leadership positions across sectors (nonprofit, municipal and federal governments). In the early 2000s, she became the chief of staff for the New York City Department of Youth and Community Development. After, Lisette was the founding executive director of Year Up, the national workforce development program for young people (see Noel Anderson's story in Chapter 2). Barack Obama appointed Lisette to the White House Initiative on Educational Excellence for Hispanics.

Lisette advises everyone to try and realize the power they have regardless of what position they hold. Even the smallest act can reap big help to those facing struggles related to inequity. She says we must believe that "your best work is not the work you do, it's done through others. That's your best work, where you can be of value. You have to be willing to disrupt, be uncomfortable, and make things uncomfortable. I'm proud of my dad for that. I got it early: 'There's only so far obedience is going to get you.'"

Nothing to Lose: The Institution Is More Afraid Than You Are

STORYTELLER:
Former student body president of a CUNY junior college and CUNY four-year college

"I am the primary source of my family's income," says Bazen Abate. A recent college graduate, Bazen has shouldered more responsibility than most people his age, especially when it comes to other people's burdens. Bazen was born and raised in Gambia, West Africa. At seventeen, Bazen left Gambia, "a really poor country without many opportunities to earn a living income," for Spain, a route he chose because it made immigrating to the US slightly easier.

Within eight months of leaving his homeland, in the summer of 2017, Bazen had a visa to travel to the US. He landed in the South Bronx of New York City and immediately secured a job at a car wash, as well as housing with a group of other young immigrant men. "I came to work and to provide for my family back home, but I also realized I needed to go to school because I couldn't read or write in English," Bazen says. He enrolled at the South Bronx's International Community High School, where all students are immigrants. Bazen found a strong community at International Community High.

"I learned early on to advocate for myself," Bazen says. Most students were Spanish speakers; only a few came from African countries, and those were French-speaking countries, unlike Bazen's Gambia. Bazen volunteered whenever possible to gain important experiences and be of service. Despite his busy schedule with work, Bazen often represented the school at community functions and events. As he settled in at school, he heard from his teachers, school administrators, and counselors, "You are gifted. You should continue your education after you finish high school." "I was lucky because my principal saw me as someone deserving of the opportunity to go to college," Bazen says.

Bazen knew furthering his education would be difficult. In addition to going to school full-time, he would have to continue working full-time. He began working at a restaurant, and though this was less labor-intensive than the car wash job, he often worked from 5 p.m. to 2 or 3 a.m. He went to school most days after three or four hours of sleep. "My eyes were red. You could see it. It was hard to focus." On top of these stressors, Bazen's family wanted him to quit school to work more hours and earn more money. "In our communities, there's an expectation [to take care of your family]. Don't get me wrong, it's a beautiful expectation—I don't want to see my family suffering back home." Bazen was one of ten siblings back in Gambia.

But Bazen knew education was the better path to a family-sustaining livelihood, even if it meant working himself to the bone. He was accepted to four-year colleges, but he knew his best bet was to attend a community college to continue strengthening his English. Because Bazen was undocumented and ineligible for federal student aid, he applied to a junior college which was part of the City University of New York (CUNY), and received its full-ride Immigrant Scholarship[2].

Bazen started school while working grueling hours on UberEats. This was also during the peak of the pandemic when most schools held only online classes. "I noticed that me and many other [low-income and immigrant] students needed to borrow Wi-Fi hotspots at home. We also needed laptops. Laptops are expensive. I couldn't afford it, and [I know] many other students couldn't afford it." Bazen decided to run for student government president at this CUNY junior college. His platform largely revolved around increasing student access to technology necessary to achieve academically. Bazen ran a vibrant online campaign and won the election.

"Becoming president increased my passion for advocacy significantly," Bazen says. His new perch offered a view into how other students experienced marginalization. Bazen found that Muslim students were not afforded the same privileges as non-Muslims. "I [began to] notice that we observed many holidays—Christian religious holidays, Jewish religious holidays—but there was no Eid holiday for us [Muslim students]. CUNY has a significant Muslim population. I wrote a letter to the Chancellor's office demanding Eid holiday be observed for Muslim students."

After securing his associate's degree, Bazen was accepted to an elite four-year college within the CUNY network—to complete his bachelor's. This college's student population was larger and more visible. With newfound confidence, Bazen decided to run for student government president again at this new college. He was an independent candidate going up against an incumbent. Part of his platform was to formalize Eid observance across CUNY schools. He won his race.

Weeks before Bazen's college graduation in the spring of 2024, CUNY announced that Muslim students for the first time would be granted Eid observance beginning in the spring of 2025. Though Bazen himself would not officially enjoy the holiday as a student of the system, the event would solidify his legacy. "I can say I've been student president of two CUNY schools," Bazen says. "That's something I'm proud of because as an immigrant student, it's not something I could

---

[2] These colleges have been de-identified to protect Bazen's identity.

have ever imagined for myself." But he also recognizes and quickly lists all the people who also fought for Muslim representation and Eid commemoration.

While Bazen's story could end there, it doesn't. Bazen is not a person who simply speaks about advocacy.

"In this political context, it has been exhausting serving as an undergraduate student government president at this college," Bazen says, referring to events following the October 7, 2023, massacre of Israeli citizens and the subsequent genocide of Palestinians in Gaza. That fall, the CUNY Chancellor, Felix Matos Rodriguez, called students who protested Israel's war "terrorist sympathizers," and one-sided rhetoric from the school's highest leadership continued.

Bazen sprang into action. He created a group chat with student body presidents of all CUNY campuses. He then authored a letter to Chancellor Matos Rodriguez, which was signed by each of the student presidents, urging the chancellor to equally condemn anti-Muslim and Islamic bigotry and dehumanization of Palestinians. The students also requested a meeting. "If he denied meeting with us, we could go public with it," Bazen said confidently, as if a longtime veteran at high-stakes politics.

Matos Rodriguez's office agreed to a meeting with the students but scheduled it for finals week. Still a substantial contingent of the presidents arrived. They asked Matos Rodriguez to protect student protestors and their freedom of speech. Bazen also warned the administration that if CUNY continued to oppose the protestors, the demonstrations would likely grow. "We could see the encampment coming. I almost begged [the chancellor] to make a public statement [expressing sympathy for both sides]. It would be symbolic if he did." The chancellor listened intently but did not agree to the student presidents' demands.

Then, in April 2024, just as Bazen and his peers had warned, a student encampment formed at the City College of New York in West Harlem. Despite the protest being peaceful, Matos Rodriguez requested that the NYPD disband the camp. Immediately, Bazen sent another letter to the Chancellor. "We are able to point out a CUNY Board of Trustees Policy #7.071 which says, in an event where CUNY is to ever call in the NYPD [against students], they have to consult the student trustees and the University Student Senate."

Bazen made his way to the encampment, and while he live-streamed the event, police grabbed him from behind. He was arrested and handcuffed. Bazen was released early the next morning and not charged.

Bazen had a lot to lose by acting so boldly on his convictions, but he doesn't see it that way. He sees himself as a servant. "I made a vow to advocate for the students. When you genuinely care . . . there's no fear that can stop [you]. That's how I feel. . . . The fear actually comes from [the] institution. In this [situation], even the chancellor is scared. He's scared he might lose his job. Me, I'm majoring in political science and international relations. How do I surrender to institutional pressure? I'm not that kind of person. I don't think that way."

Choosing Wellness Over Achievement Cures the Crisis of Courage
STORYTELLER: JEFF DUNCAN-ANDRADE

Jeff Duncan-Andrade completed his PhD at UC Berkeley and his postdoctoral training at UCLA, a path usually leading straight into a tenure-track professorship at a prestigious university. Instead, Jeff took his credentials and talents to the newly opened East Oakland Community High School as an English teacher. The school was modeled after the Black Panthers' Oakland-based Liberation Schools of the 1970s.

At East Oakland Community High, Jeff ran a program called Step to College in which twenty-five high school students enrolled at the local campus San Francisco State University to take advanced courses. Sadly, the Oakland Unified School District shut down the school when the program's students were high school juniors. This was during the "small schools" movement of the early 2000s. The district had no plans for where these students would complete their senior year, even though "92% of these kids were going to go on to four-year schools," Jeff says. "Nobody would touch us because we were too politically hot." Eventually, a charter school with low enrollment agreed to register the East Oakland students as its own. Jeff and his class had to meet at their former building, then drive across the city to their new school, where they started an hour early with Step to College, every day, during their senior year.

Later, at a graduation party, a group of students and families, including two female students with newborn babies, approached Jeff. "They said, 'We want you to start a school that starts in kindergarten, so our children can have the same thing that you gave us. But [it has to be] all the way through, because we lost too many of our friends before they got to ninth grade. It has to start earlier.'" Having never taught elementary school, Jeff was initially reluctant: "Actually, I never wanted to open a school." But in the years that followed, the idea of opening a school premised on the young women's suggestion gnawed at him.

Jeff started teaching a new cohort of thirty freshmen the next year at Fremont High School. He guided the students in year-long research projects in a unit called "Doc Your Block," whose purpose was to document neighborhoods through ethnographic and participatory action research. They designed projects to determine what needed transformation in their community and how they might achieve it. Starting in ninth grade and through their senior year, the students interrogated what their ideal teachers would look like, what their ideal school would look like, and what their ideal community would look like.

Armed with insights from these projects (along with his learnings from a transformational visit to Maori Indigenous schools in New Zealand), Jeff now had a blueprint for opening a school for students *by* students. He could not put off the request made by his female students, past and present. Jeff describes the development of his vision:

> What is the purpose of this public-school project in a society that ... has said that it is committed to becoming a pluralistic multiracial democracy but that in reality is the most radically unequal society in the history of the industrialized world? [If we don't start] truth telling and having a conversation about what is the role of public schools in course correcting, I think we're in trouble ... Our effort at [our school] Roses in Concrete was to begin to wrestle with that question as a community and to investigate a vision and a mission and an implementation of a school-wide institutional commitment to saying that the purpose of public schools in this society, and frankly in any society, should be the wellness of children. Period ... full stop.

Jeff says that understanding what wellness looks like requires understanding a necessary distinction between "apology" and "atonement."

On the playground, if a child hurts another child physically or verbally, they are taught to apologize, after which all parties move on. "This scales up," Jeff says. "This is what we see from our leaders now, is that they apologize and they move on." But, according to Jeff, the hurt hasn't ceased to exist. "What I want to see in schools in connection with this commitment to wellness, is atonement, which includes apology—you [have] got to acknowledge that you did harm. Then when that child comes back the next day, you have to pour extra medicine in, there's a debt due because [they were] harmed."

Further, Jeff asserts that acknowledging, recognizing, and tending to children's wellness is difficult if we do not measure it in academic settings. "We measure reading scores because that's what matters to us. That's the problem . . . there is no academic rigor without wellness."

Without such action, reflection, and then reaction, Jeff says it becomes impossible for anyone in a school to be well. Health data on school professionals and students shows how frighteningly bad mental health is within our school spaces. Educational leaders must advocate for school practices that uphold everyone's wellness as a core value, especially for schools in underserved communities such as Roses in Concrete, where unmeasurable but significant nonacademic challenges and forms of intergenerational trauma may affect children. Jeff plans to send his own twin boys to the school in their elementary years.

For Jeff, the most rewarding experience from this project has been the daily student school drop-off, and the first day of school in the inaugural year was the most powerfully emotional. Having been a schoolteacher for most of his career, Jeff says he had never fully understood the significance of drop-off until that day. "It moved me to tears to watch my community bring their babies to the doorstep of the school we started to build. . . . You see that this [young] child is nearly fully dependent on this parent or caregiver who hands them over to us and turns their back to walk away . . . This sacred moment is [often] ignored in schools, the significance of it, and what it means for a parent or a caregiver to send their child to us." If school professionals would reflect on the importance of such sacred moments like school drop-off, they might be better prepared to serve their students and communities from a wellness and human-centered standpoint.

Jeff believes that the intention to restore humanity to teaching requires bravery:

> This nation is profoundly unjust, unequal, and inequitable, but there's a growing awareness about that... But there's also a crisis of courage in the nation and all the way across the field of education. For the better part of my adult life, I've wanted to be the kind of educator, leader, community member, parent, friend, partner that found the courage to tell the truth and then sort out what that truth means. When people find the courage to step out, humble themselves, and become a truth teller, and [when they] get proximate to pain, they're often doing it in isolation of their broader community of educational leaders. That, inevitably, can lead to a new crisis of courage or at least a crisis of sustainability, like how long can you actually do that totally on your own?

The goal is to build educational spaces where courage is inherent in the culture and climate. That way, our students will not only have worthy examples to follow as they change the world but also create a cohesive community while they do it. As they develop courage, they do so collectively.

Chapter Summary

This chapter's stories showcase the importance of centering human dignity in any educational leadership pursuit. Each person's potential is deserving of consideration. Here are some of the primary themes across these stories.

Believing In All People Is an Insurgent Mindset and Requires Bravery

The educational ecosystem has some unequal distribution of resources and outcomes—for both students and stakeholders. This encourages the perception that some people are more worthy and deserving than others, which reinforces existing inequitable structures. This means that believing in *all* people—believing that your students have what it takes to go to college or believing that your father can learn to read and write—requires bravery and confidence.

The academic field of educational leadership could place more emphasis on this belief. The existing research and scholarship in educational leadership focuses heavily on management and operations. But managing and operating schools, budgets, and staffing does little to improve the status quo.

Leadership means going against these deeply rooted beliefs, cultures, and ideologies and championing the idea that everyone, in their own way, is brilliant. No one is simply the sum of their past actions, mistakes, and adverse circumstances; nay, what defines us is how we prevail over these tribulations. Like the storytellers in these chapters, our leadership can demonstrate that all people—and *especially* all children—are worthy of forgiveness, reparation, and deliverance. Some, like Jeff Duncan-Andrade, see this path forged through atonement; others, like Lisette Nieves, see it in the offering of red lipstick to a dying patient. Whatever it looks like for you to believe in everyone, do it.

To make meaningful positive change in education, we must realize that our work is *insurgent*. We have to disrupt and not manage the status quo. Injustices are abound: a price-gouging landlord; the private standardized testing industry that neglects student wellness; a university leader who sends in the city's police department to disband his own, peacefully protesting students; some children never learning to read. And as Jennifer Blanchette does, we must remind others that they cannot simply complain about social problems without also supporting efforts toward establishing a brighter future.

The world does not *have to* be this way. We must all be activists and abolitionists to catalyze a stronger, more equitable system for all.

Successful Educational Leadership Is Approached Through Joy

Education can be hard work in discouraging circumstances. If we internalize the problems, we become disheartened and unable to motivate and lead others. Effective leadership necessitates that we maintain our joy. (Even rebels need nourishment and love.) At each turn, we must remember what it was that brought us to this work. Facilitating a child's love of reading is joyous. Watching parents push down their anxieties and drop their children off at school is inspiring. Advocating for the basic funding that students deserve, and winning it, is triumphant.

We must celebrate these wins together. Joy is multiplied in the company of others, a solidarity iron-clad and unshakable.

No matter the challenges you encounter, solutions are always to be found—sometimes where we least expect them. To promote an educational system that serves everyone, we must remove the limits that constrain us from achieving our vision. That is pragmatic optimism. I hope that the stories you have read in this book affirm for you that you are on the right path.

Though the terrain may be tough, you are tougher. Arm yourself with a positive outlook as well as the allyship of others and you will get where you aspire to go.

CONCLUSION

Education Needs All of Us to Be Leaders

The war against public education and academic freedom is going strong.[1] Given the trajectory we are on, there is a significant chance that this book will be banned in the same state where I wrote it. It is becoming the norm to censor content that promotes social justice principles.

In June of 2024, I was invited to give the Keynote Address at the Broward County Public Schools Academic Enrichment Conference. Broward County neighbors Miami and represents the second largest school district in Florida and the sixth largest in the United States. I was excited to give a talk in my backyard, where many of my FIU students and colleagues live and commute from.

But before the event organizers could approve my presentation or purchase a bulk order of my first book, *The Power of Student Agency*, for the audience, I and my work were "audited." In sum, organizers had to ensure that there were no problematic keywords in my writing, including but not limited to the terms "systemic racism"[2] or "white supremacy." Ultimately, it was deemed that my book and I passed this exam. Honestly, that outcome was surprising to me to a degree. And

---

[1] Jack Schneider and Jennifer Berkshire, *Education Wars: A Citizen's Guide and Defense Manual* (The New Press, 2024).

[2] I do however use "*structural* racism" on two occasions. I don't know whether they searched for that keyword.

during that process I kept thinking about how *this* book—the one I was writing at the time—certainly would not meet those same standards. And honestly, I'm proud if it does not.

This is the shaky state of education today, an arena that finds itself squarely in the middle of the increasingly hostile contemporary culture war. Following Trump's return to the presidency, tensions are high. Public schools are constantly at the center of political debate, vilified by conservatives who champion for "school choice" while discrediting public schools and those who work in them in the name of "educational reform." Florida is typically front and center in such news—the belly of the beast if you will, consistently advancing legislation that seems intent to delegitimize, defund, and destabilize the public school system.

Across the country, governments are following Florida's lead. One policy here allows public funds to be drained as families pull out public dollars for use in private education vouchers. Some of these families would have sent their kids to private schools regardless of these financial incentives, only hurting public infrastructure for their own private needs. There are other threats against critical sources of public funding, such as Title I and its many protections and affordances for poor families.

And rather than focus on what students in schools need, we seemingly focus excessively on buzzwords and headline issues, such as the appropriateness of gender inclusive restrooms. Meanwhile, there have been physical brawls at school board meetings and classroom libraries have been covered up by tarps by uneasy teachers or completely emptied by administrators for containing "controversial" books.

Educators struggle to locate, harness, and unleash their own agency to the betterment of their students. Record numbers flee the teaching profession altogether, and we have an alarming, national teacher shortage crisis throughout our public school systems as classrooms remain underfunded and overcrowded.

We are left to wonder: Who will serve these students?

The most glaring issue to me is one of framing: public education has been strategically pitted as the *problem* when in fact it should be upheld as the *solution*. Through education we could ease the stresses of catastrophic climate change, diminishing social security, the automation of jobs and activities, senseless mass incarceration, and general malaise.

Even many of us being unable to function happily without our phones could also be remedied through education.

Research corroborates that most of the general public believes in the public good that public education provides.[3] But politics keeps standing in the way. Schools are being used to divide us even farther along arbitrary lines when instead they should be used to bring us together.

This book, which directly speaks to the promotion of *equity* in and around schools in order to serve *all* students, might rightfully be contested in this context. I am grateful to readers like you who, if you made it this far, are unwilling to let the status quo define and dictate your journey and intention to lead in education. I remain in awe of educational leaders from John B. King to Debra Bazile who put themselves on the line to support their students; they realize that while the establishment may have its own agenda, we cannot let it deter us from *ours*. We need more hands-on deck now than ever before to correct the course of education and democratize it to the fullest extent possible. This is the challenge of our lifetime.

If you take away something—anything—from this book, let it be this: the status quo is specifically engineered to make us believe we are powerless against it as well as the larger forces that be. That is by design. For us to create better and fairer systems for all, we have to actively unlearn some of what we have become conditioned to believe in order to create novel frameworks of possibility for ourselves and others to follow. We have to have a hopeful imagination.

After all, it comes more naturally to simply identify and observe a problem—like in-school racialized tracking or between-school segregation—and move on than it is to believe you can *do* something about it. We worry we have no agency in a world chock-full of structural challenges.

We have been conditioned to believe that we can only achieve our aims within the confines of what we see; and in the case of education, we are mostly preoccupied by noticing and dealing with restraints and limitations. But there are new horizons of possibilities to be obtained, even if they have not been obtained yet.

---

[3] Jack Schneider and Jennifer Berkshire, *A Wolf at the Schoolhouse Door: The Dismantling of Public Education and the Future of School* (The New Press, 2020).

The stories in this book have highlighted ways for us to expand beyond these confines. They teach us that our ability to promote greater equity requires having a healthy dose of imagination as well as steady conviction to see our dreams through. In essence, we have to nurture our inner children, where is lodged the belief that reality can be shaped more than it shapes us.

Following my keynote in Broward in the fall of 2024, I gave a talk at an education and tech company, one of the largest US-based providers of teaching and learning materials for schools across K-12 and higher education. The company was interested in supporting student and staff agency. My routine tone and approach had shifted to becoming more active and assertive as I called on the audience to create more equitable conditions for both students and themselves to take control of their learning contexts.

At the end of my lecture and during the Q and A, a woman asked, "Dr. Kundu, it seems as if you're just a breath away from advocating for agency giving way to activism; that is, [people] and their learning communities not only taking control of the *content* but the *context* of their education. What does this look like to you, mindful that an 'activist' does not necessarily equal a 'revolutionary'?"

"What's wrong with being a revolutionary?" I replied. "Maybe that's a valid goal we should set for our students. After all, the world they are growing up in is anything but justified in its current format." Agency and activism are two sides of the same coin.

The time for us to be passive has long passed. Education was never meant to have us acquiesce to our surroundings, but rather liberate us from the oppressive systems limiting our potential.

We must remember that ideology disguises itself as common sense. It is common sense today that a Black child is lawfully entitled to be literate, but it was not common sense in our great-grandparents' time. But great-grandparents, radicals, and revolutionaries dared to challenge the status quo and believe in a more inclusive society. If they hadn't, hearts and minds would not have been converted, common sense would not have aligned with the times.

Together we must be radical. We can tackle gargantuan challenges such as school segregation, but the way to embark on that path is to start like Denise Williamson did—small and local, sharpening our own locus of control before branching out and supporting each other. In these ways, no ambition is too large, from dismantling the school-to-prison pipeline and mass incarceration, to eliminating school shootings and ushering in national gun control reform.

After all, as go the schools, so goes the society.

We should begin with the premise that everyone is needed, in each their unique capacities, to be educational leaders. We need to dismantle our rigid notions of leadership, embracing ideas of inclusivity and interconnectedness. We must expand leadership, including as many partners and co-conspirators as possible, recognizing all actions and efforts as important, and realizing what we are capable of when we push beyond our limits and preconceived notions. We can create an educational system that is an antidote to our larger social problems.

Our future depends on us doing so.

I am forever grateful for educational leaders like Denise Williamson who stare injustice in the face and dare to persevere. They are heroes. I am humbled to have been able to tell some of their stories here.

THE EDUCATIONAL LEADERSHIP FOR EQUITY TOOLKIT

CO-DEVELOPED WITH DR. LILLIAN SCHENCK, NEW YORK CITY PUBLIC SCHOOLS TOOLKIT

This section offers a reflective companion to the vignettes encountered throughout the book. It is a versatile guide crafted to help you delve deeper into the principles of equity we have investigated and apply this book's lessons in your everyday leadership journey.

The toolkit is structured to facilitate a personalized and thoughtful examination of each chapter's insights. However, given that the best learning is often collaborative, it can be more meaningful to complete toolkit exercises with peers or teams and then review them in community. Treat the toolkit according to your needs—whether that means revisiting key themes, exploring reflective prompts, or connecting ideas to your unique educational contexts.

The toolkit is not meant to surface plain summaries of what you've learned but rather insights into how you might apply that knowledge to spark and enhance your growth as an equitable leader.

Chapter 1 Toolkit

The Sociology of Leading Systems Change

Reflective Journal	
Activity: Keep a reflective journal for one week on how social reproduction (see "Functionalist and Conflict Perspectives	**Reflection Prompts** At the end of the week, review your journal entries.

Continued

Continued

Inform Grounded Leadership"). Look for areas where the school's influence might be reinforcing inequities rather than challenging them. when you notice inequalities being reproduced (e.g., through funding disparities, disciplinary practices, curriculum choices). Document your observations and your emotional responses to these moments.	• What patterns or themes do you see? • How do these observations challenge or reinforce your understanding of your role as an educational leader? • What actions can you take to disrupt these patterns and promote a more equitable educational environment?

Equity and Inclusion Audit

Activity: Audit your school's policies and practices regarding equity and inclusion. Reflect on how your school addresses systemic inequalities (see "Educational Leaders Maintain Our Social Fabric" and "Functionalist and Conflict Perspectives"	**Action Prompts** • Create a detailed report based on your findings. Include an action plan outlining specific steps your leadership team can take to promote equity and create a more inclusive environment for all students and staff. • Present your findings to your leadership team or to a group of peers and discuss how to implement these changes.

Personal Agency Mapping

Activity: Reflect on your journey as an educational leader by creating a visual map of your personal agency. Identify key moments in your career when you exercised agency and how those moments shaped your path (see "Fostering Agency and Mobilizing Forms of Capital as a Guiding Theoretical Framework"). Include the forms of social and cultural capital that supported you during those times. Share your map with a peer and discuss how these experiences have influenced your leadership style and decision-making.	**Reflection Prompts** • On the basis of your map, has your understanding of your agency evolved over time? How? • What forms of social and cultural capital most influenced your journey, and how can you leverage these resources to support others in your school community?

Chapter 2 Toolkit
Build Better Systems: Address Students' and Stakeholders' Basic Needs

System Mapping to Build a Better System	
Activity: Select a system or process in your school or organization that you believe could be improved to better meet the basic needs of students and stakeholders. Sketch out a before and after map of this system. In the before section, identify the gaps or inefficiencies, and in the after section, propose changes inspired by the stories in Chapter 2.	**Reflection Prompt** • How would your proposed changes create a more supportive and resilient system? • Consider the roles of collaboration, resource allocation, and individual empowerment in your redesign.

Role Reversal Dialogue	
Activity: Imagine a conversation between your current self and a teacher, mentor, or leader from your past who significantly influenced your life, much like Mr. Osterweil did for John B. King Jr. ("Safe, but stretched"). In this dialogue, explore how that person's actions and values shaped your approach to leadership today. Write out this dialogue, alternating between your perspective and theirs.	**Reflection Prompt** • How can you embody the qualities of that mentor in your current role to create a lasting impact on the lives of those you lead?

Get Proximate	
Activity: Spend a day shadowing a student, teacher, or staff member from your institution, focusing on understanding their daily challenges and triumphs (see "Offer High Expectations and High Support by Getting More Proximate").	**Reflection Prompts** • What surprised you about your subject's daily reality? • How did this experience change your perspective on the challenges they face? • How will this proximity influence your future decisions as a leader? • What steps will you take to ensure your leadership remains connected to the needs of those you serve?

Chapter 3 Toolkit

Make Sense of the Nonsensical: Apply Research to Unearth and Solve Injustices

Ethnographic Storytelling	
Activity: To gain a deeper understanding of how inequities manifest in daily educational practices and environments, conduct brief interviews or informal conversations with a diverse group of stakeholders in your educational community (e.g., students, teachers, parents, support staff). Collect stories that reveal instances of inequity or social justice challenges (see "Fix Something Unfair? That's What I Do All Day" and "Closing Schools... Equitably").	**Reflection Prompts** • What themes or patterns emerged from the stories you collected? • How do these narratives challenge or confirm your understanding of the systemic issues in your school or district? • How can these stories inform your approach to leadership and policymaking? • Does one pattern stand out as a candidate for more investigation? What data could you gather to help you devise a solution?
Mapping Power and Influence	
Activity: To explore the dynamics of power, influence, and structural barriers in your educational environment, create a visual map of it. Highlight the stakeholders, power structures, and systemic barriers that influence decision-making and the approach to promoting equity. Use symbols, colors, and annotations to represent elements such as resource distribution, cultural tensions, and policy influences.	**Reflection Prompts** • Where do you see the most significant barriers to equity in your environment? • Who holds the power to break down these barriers, and how can that power be leveraged for positive change? • Do your values and leadership style make sense within this map? Are there areas where you can take action or advocate for change?
Personal Reflection Timeline	
Activity: Create a timeline of your educational career, marking significant moments where you faced challenging decisions or situations. Reflect on how your personal experiences shaped your approach to leadership (see "Closing Schools... Equitably" or "There's Room at the Table for All of Us").	**Reflection Prompts** • Do your past experiences influence your perspective on dealing with controversial or emotionally charged issues? • How can you use these experiences to foster a more empathetic and research-driven approach in your current role?

- What kinds of evidence or data can help to bring people onto your side, especially those who seem resistant to your ideas, by appealing to their emotions and values?

Chapter 4 Toolkit

Stick to Your Guns: Lead with Values, Conviction, and Information

Legacy Vision Board

Activity: Make a vision board that represents the leadership legacy you wish to create. Include images, quotes, and symbols that reflect your core values and the changes you aspire to make in education. Include the formative people who have informed your vision. They can be historic figures such as W. E. B DuBois or people in your network.

Reflection Prompts

- Write a reflection on how well your personal values align with your professional goals.
- What actions will you take to stay resilient in the face of adversity?
- Share your vision board and reflection with a mentor or colleague for additional insights.

Dialogue with a Hypothetical Ally

Activity: In a creative role-playing exercise, simulate a conversation with a hypothetical ally or supporter.

1. Choose an ongoing challenge or goal related to your leadership role.
2. Imagine an ally who possesses the exact skills, knowledge, or influence needed to help you. Describe this ally in detail.
3. Write or record a dialogue between yourself and this ally discussing the challenge, exploring solutions, and negotiating support.

Reflection Prompts

- How did envisioning this ally's perspective influence your understanding of the challenge?
- What strategies or approaches emerged that you hadn't considered before?
- What insights did you gain that might apply to your real-world situation?

Continued

Continued

Historical and Future Advocacy Letter	
Activity: Write two letters: one to a past version of yourself and another to a future version of yourself. 1. **Letter to the past**: Offer advice and insights to yourself at an earlier point in your career on the basis of the resilience and advocacy themes from the chapter. 2. **Letter to the future**: Envision how you, five to ten years from now, will continue to advocate for equity and resilience, and what you hope to have achieved.	**Reflection Prompts** • How do the insights from the chapter help shape your vision for the future, your advocacy and leadership? • What guidance can you offer to your past self, and what aspirations do you have for your future leadership journey?

Chapter 5 Toolkit

Hand-Ups Over Handouts: Promote Agency Above All Else

Hand-Up vs. Handout Workshop	
Activity: Organize a workshop where participants break into small groups to analyze case studies or real-life scenarios related to student support and empowerment. The analyses involve a choice between providing a temporary aid (handout) and a supportive, empowering intervention (hand-up). Groups discuss the potential impacts of each approach and present their findings. Conclude with a group discussion on how to implement more hand-up strategies in each participant's school or program.	**Reflection Prompts** • How did the hand-up approach in your case studies differ from traditional methods of aid? • What are the potential long-term benefits of fostering self-sufficiency among students?

Agency Mapping Exercise

Activity: Create a large visual map or infographic that illustrates how students can navigate their educational journey with agency. Include elements such as available resources, support systems, and potential barriers. Invite participants to contribute their own ideas and solutions for strengthening student agency. Include in the map pathways that empower students to make decisions and take control of their learning and future.

Reflection Prompts
- What resources or supports does your map have that are currently not available to students?
- How can you remove the barriers you identified to student agency in your educational setting?

Future Vision Storytelling

Activity: Imagine it's ten years from now, and you're reflecting on a successful initiative or program you led in your current role. Write a short story or create a narrative presentation that describes how your leadership has transformed your educational environment and affected the community. Include key achievements, unexpected challenges overcome, and the ways your leadership has fostered empowerment and resilience among students and stakeholders.

Reflection Prompts
- How does your vision align with the strategies and values demonstrated by the storytellers in this chapter? Who in particular does your vision align strongly with?
- What specific actions or decisions in your narrative were inspired by the stories of these leaders?
- What insights did you gain about your leadership's effects and the potential they had for systemic change? What steps can you take now to make this vision a reality?

Chapter 6 Toolkit

Center Human Dignity: Champion All People's Right to Receive a Transformative Education

Courageous Change Proposal

Activity: Develop a proposal for courageous change for your educational setting. Choose one of the experiences in this chapter that could

Reflection Prompt
- Why would advancing your proposal require bravery? What forces might try to work against you?

Continued

Continued

be adapted to your setting, and then outline a proposal for a new initiative or policy in your school or organization that embodies courageous leadership with a focus on human dignity. Be sure to address the following in your proposal:

- The specific issue or need it tackles.
- The values of advocacy and wellness, discussed in the chapter.
- The implementation steps and how to measure its impact.

- Share your proposal with a mentor or colleague for additional insights. Incorporate their feedback and perspectives as you improve on your plan's design.

Human Dignity Role-Play

Activity: Organize a role-play exercise where each participant assumes the perspective of a different stakeholder involved in a major education reform initiative, such as student, parent, teacher, policymaker, or community leader. Role-play scenarios where these stakeholders debate and discuss the importance of centering human dignity in educational policies and practices.

Reflection Prompts

- Ask participants how their character's perspective shaped their stance on human dignity in education.
- What were the main conflicts or challenges that arose during the debate?
- How did the role-play help you understand the importance of advocating for human dignity in your leadership practice?

Collaborative Storytelling Workshop

Activity: Organize a collaborative storytelling workshop where participants share stories that highlight the importance of human dignity in education, basing them on real events or hypothetical scenarios. Include the types of challenges and successes described in the chapter. Encourage participants to work in groups to develop their stories and present them to the larger group.

Reflection Prompts

- Did collaborating on these stories help participants gain new perspectives on upholding human dignity?
- What themes or insights emerged from the stories?
- How can storytelling inform your approach to leadership and advocacy for human dignity in your educational context?

ACKNOWLEDGMENTS

By the second time you write a book, you've learned a thing or two. For me, most importantly, I learned that I needed help. A lot of it. I'm incredibly fortunate to have some of these world-class people support me on this project.

Thank you to the Oxford University Press team for supporting me soundly and kindly through quite a rigorous process. Peer review is not for the faint of heart! Special thanks to Hayley Singer, a wonderful and thoughtful editor, for all your guidance and partnership through this process. A sincere thank you as well to James Cook for seeing the potential in this project early on and choosing to not let it go.

Thank you to the esteemed Prudence Carter, a scholar who I look up to because of her kindness, grace, and criticality, for writing such a poignant and thought-provoking foreword.

Thank you, so much, to Jenn Bennett-Genthner for always helping edit my work at a moment's notice, and for also introducing me to Mary Ann Short, a dream developmental editor. Thank you, Mary Ann, for your directness and shaping this book to make more sense than it would have without you.

An enormous thank you to Gabby Portela for helping streamline my processes and being so on-the-ball that I made my deadlines. Special thanks also to Jason Le, for your enthusiasm and collaboration, as well as the ideas you brought to the table. Thank you, Lillian Schenck, for your enthusiasm and contributions despite having such a full plate. Thank you to Ella Webb, for playing an important role in helping me set the initial groundwork for this project to take off. Special thanks to additional helpers Becca Huntting, Meghna Laha, and Hiya Banerjee for their close reads of this work.

I would also like to give a heartfelt thanks to my colleagues at FIU in the College of Arts, Sciences, and Education, who are consummately supportive and encouraging. In particular, thank you to Dan Saunders, Kris Ugarte-Torre, and Courtney

Rose for being the best colleagues a guy could have. Thank you, Zahra Hazari for your brilliant mentorship; Aaron Kuntz for your supportive leadership; Kirsten Edwards for your solidarity and guidance.

I must thank my family for cheerleading me through this journey. Without you, it would have been easier to give up. Ma, Baba, Didi, thank you for your endless supply of love.

Pam, you are my rock, thanks for always believing in me and making life worth living. Jai and Mika: you are each my whole world, and you give me more than you will ever know.

Finally, a major and most important thank you to the participants of this project. Without your stories and time, there would be no book. I am honored to have been able to give your experiences another stage and I hope there are more to come.

And thank you to anyone else reading this—you make this work fulfilling. You have more power than you know.

INDEX

Tables, figures and boxes are indicated by an italic *t*, *f*, and *b* following the page number.
For the benefit of digital users, indexed terms that span two pages (e.g., 52–53) may, on occasion, appear on only one of those pages.

AAPI-LEAD Youth Conference, 125–126
Abbott, Greg, 145–146
accountability, educational leadership, 35–37
achievement
 assessments on, 17
 challenge of notion, 51
 importance for all, 30–32
 interventionist approach, 85
achievement gap
 public education, 120
 racial, 69
achievement-opportunity gap, Black-white, 104
activism, social justice and, 127
adversity, leaders in, 111
affluence, segregation of, 15–16
African Americans, Du Bois on, 112–113
agency
 definition of, 33–35
 education leaders, 65–66
 educators, 179
 foundational concept of, 62
 individual, 33–35
 mapping exercise, 188*t*
 personal, mapping, 183*t*
 person's individual, 137
 perspective in education, 61
 psychology and social factors, 62
 reducing barriers to promote, 151–152
 teacher leveraging own, 59–61
AIDS infections, 167
Alice in Wonderland, 77
Alonzo A. Crim Center for Urban Education Excellence (CUEE), 142
Alzheimer's, 75
American, scope of being, 44
American Enterprise Institute, 115
American Library Association, 45

American Sociological Association, 101–102, 105
AmeriCorps, 167
Anderson, Noel S., 70, 89
    The Perfect Storm and a Yellow Sweater (storyteller), 78–81
    yellow sweater in story, 80–81, 89
Anyon, Jean, 10
AP European history books, 82–83, 86
Aristotle, 38
Arizona, Tucson's Mexican American Studies program, 45
"armchair" expertise
    Michelangelo's masterpiece, David, 43
    teaching, 44
Asian American(s), 124, 133
Asian American, Native Hawaiian, and Pacific Islander (AANHPI), 124–127, 133
Asian American Student Advocacy Project (ASAP), 125–127, 134
Association of Community College Trustees, 96
Atlanta Public Schools (APS), 118
attention deficit disorder, 50

Bank Street College, 91
Bank Street School, 108
Bazile, Debra, 59
    For the Love of Books (storyteller), 160–163
    images from classroom, 60*f*
    structure-agency dichotomy, 58–62
Bazile, Mauratus, 160–162
belief, educating people, 155
belonging, empowering others, 153–154
Benjamin, Ruha, 31–32
Bezos, Jeff, 51
Black Panthers, 172

Black students, expectations, 20
Blanchette, Jennifer, 176
    The Mother of All (storyteller), 163–165
Bloomberg, Michael, 115, 121–124, 159
books
    bans in Florida, 45
    opportunity gap, 59–61
    storyteller promoting literacy, 160–163
bravery
    believing in all people, 175–176
    restoring humanity to teaching, 175
Brewer, Jan, 45
Brockton High School, Wolder, 82
Brockton Public Schools, Wolder, 82–85
Brookings Institution, 116
Brooklyn College, 167
Broward County Public Schools Academic Enrichment Conference, 178
Brown University, 91, 94, 101–106
Brown v. Board of Education (1954), 14, 128
Burdick, Jake, 10
Bush, George H. W., 116
Bush, George W., No Child Left Behind (NCLB) law, 115

Caballero, Judge, 147
California, schools "hemorrhaging educators" in, 159
capitalist ideology, 69
capitalist society, schooling in, 52
Carter, Prudence, 106–107, 109
    There's Room at the Table for All of Us (storyteller), 101–106
    wealth and poverty, 107–108
Cashin, Sheryll, 15–16
Castro, Andrene, 10
causes and effects, questioning unfavorable, 106–107

INDEX 195

Center for the Study of Race and Ethnicity in America (CSREA), 101–106
Central Park East Elementary School, 91
CharacterLab, 73–74
charter school(s), 115
   Pedro on approach to, 123
   public and, 121–122
Charter School Authorization Committee, 120
cheating scandal, Atlanta, 118–119
Chertavain, Gerald, 78–79
Chicken Shack, 140
child poverty, 135–136
child's self-worth
   differenceness, 13–14
   giftedness, 13–14
Cho, Sumi, 53–54
Chomsky, Noam, 17
Choosing Wellness Over Achievement Cures the Crisis of Courage, Duncan-Andrade (storyteller), 172–175
Citadel (South Carolina), lawsuit against, 157–158
City College of New York, West Harlem, 171
City University of New York (CUNY), 156–160, 169–171
City Volunteer Corps, 167
classism, 14–15
Clinically Rich Teacher Preparation Programs, 76–77, 87–88
Closing Schools . . . Equitably, Malloy (storyteller), 98–101
Coalition for Asian American Children and Families (CACF), 125
cognitive behavioral therapy (CBT), 55
cognitive therapy, 73–74
collaborative research, 109–110
collective agency, education, 156

collective efficacy
   building, 68
   developing agency and, 69
   strongest indicator of student success, 67–68
   support and collaboration, 66–69
   term, 67
Columbia University, 103–104, 116
communication, leaders securing allyship, 133–134
communities
   bonds for authentic social welfare, 152–153
   challenges in relationships with members, 76
   educators' work, 44
   symbiotic relationship with schools, 43
community-engaged leadership, 100
community-minded research, Malloy, 108
community-service oriented schools, 11
comprehension, textbooks building, 83
conflict perspective
   grounded leadership, 47–57
   Marx's thesis, 49–50
connection, 88–89
Cook County Juvenile Temporary Detention Center (JTDC), 55–56
Coral Gables Senior High School, 146
cornerstone American right, access to education, 46
COVID-19 pandemic
   aftermath of, 85–86
   anti-Asian sentiments, 124–125
   data collection, 160
   dormitory and, 73
   educational leaders, 158
   family member passing away from, 167–168
   financial relief, 135–136

mental health journey, 124–125
relief fund, 126
US childhood poverty
   alleviation, 18
Create Real Economic Destiny
   (CRED), Duncan as
   partner, 138–139, 152
Crenshaw, Kimberlé, 53–54
Crim Center for Urban Education
   Excellence (CUEE), 142, 153
criminal justice, education and, 156
criminal justice system, experience
   in, 117
critical race theory (CRT), 93, 113
   Abbott ban of, 145–146
   debate on, 46
   framework, 53
cultural capital, 63
   agency of students, 69
   definition, 63
   leading by example, 88–89
   storytellers, 65
cultural competency, climate of, 11
cultural opposition theory,
   Ogbu, 103–104
culture
   achievement, 17
   encouraging equity-forward, 84
   IQ and, 18
   poverty, 17–18
Cuomo, Andrew, 124
curriculum, ethnic studies, 45

David, Michelangelo's masterpiece, 43
*Death and Life of the Great
   American School System*
   (Ravitch), 113–114, 116
Delpit, Lisa, 137, 153
   GRE program, 152
   Reducing and Removing Barriers
      to Make Way for Capable People
      (storyteller), 140–143
Delpit, Thomas, 140
desegregation, 20

public school, 127–128
Desmond, Matthew, 18
Despite the Best Intentions (Lewis and
   Diamond), 16, 20, 94, 94 n.2
Diamond, John B., 16–17, 20, 94
DianeRavitch.net, 113–114
differenceness, child's worth, 13–14
divergent thinking, equity-oriented
   leaders open to, 132–133
Donors Choose project, 162
downstream effects, 50–51
Dropout Prevention School, 163
Du Bois, W. E. B., 111–113
Duckworth, Angela, 54, 70, 88–89
   Saving Starfish (storyteller), 71–74
   student Kendra, 72, 85–87
Duncan, Arne, 137, 153
   Create Real Economic Destiny
      (CRED), 138–139, 152
   We Have to Look Out for Each
      Other (storyteller), 137–139
Duncan, Starkey, 138
Duncan, Sue, 138
Duncan-Andrade, Jeffrey, 31, 35, 176
   Choosing Wellness Over Achieve-
      ment Cures the Crisis of Courage
      (storyteller), 172–175
Durkheim, Emile, 48–49
dyslexia, 71

East Oakland Community High, 172
education
   achievement in, 17
   achieving fairness, 153
   American right to access to
      quality, 46
   conservative movement, 114
   debt affecting everyone, 19–21
   definition, 41
   formalized, 43
   improving public, 156
   insurgent mindset, 176
   leadership approach through
      joy, 176–177

leading by example, 88–89
motivation to work in, 155
open discourse on, 45
poverty and, 54
public good and universal right, 156
reducing barriers, 151–152
restoring humanity to teaching, 175
state of, 179
well-being and, 65–66
educational debt
Ladson-Billings's concept of, 20
personal level, 20–21
Educational Excellence Network, 114
educational leaders
building collective efficacy, 68
dealing with conflict, 66
educators supporting, 67
gaps between wealthy and poor, 90
goals of, 61
locus of agency and control, 65–66
maintaining social fabric, 41–46
prioritizing student success, 67
sharpening skills, 40
student demographics and, 26–27
styles, 70
task of, 57
value of, 39
educational leadership, 8–12
academic field of, 176
accountability, 35–37
approach through joy, 176–177
definitions of, 23–24
diverse storytellers, 24–27
education and management, 22–23
field, 29
formal definition, 22
knighthood of Professor of, 11–12
practitioners and scholars, 23
qualitative exploration of, 39
research strategies, 90–91
stories, 28
tenure-track professorship in, 8
theories on, 22–23

Educational Leadership for Equity Toolkit
Build Better Systems, 185t
Center Human Dignity, 189t
Hand-Ups over Handouts, 188t
Make Sense of the Nonsensical, 186t
The Sociology of Leading Systems Change, 183t
Stick to Your Guns, 187t
educational reform, 179
Teach for America (TFA), 117
educational spaces
providing capital, 64
story of "J-Stud," 64–65
education debt, 19
educators
agency of, 179
roadblocks for, 31
egalitarian ideology, public education, 54
empowering others, promoting belonging, 153–154
equity, promotion of, 180
equity and inclusion
allies for promoting, 107–109
audit, 183t
Ewing, Eve, 16–17
Expanded Child Tax Credits (CTC), 135–136
expectations, high support and, 87–88
experiences, internalizing, 13
eyeglasses, Duckworth for student, 72, 87

Fernande, Miguel, 51–52
financial aid, 103
Goldrick-Rab on college student with, 106–107
Fine, Michelle, 35
Testifying for Good (storyteller), 156–160
Finn, Chester, Jr., 114–115
First Book Marketplace, 162

Fix Something Unfair? That's What
    I Do All Day, Goldrick-Rab
    (storyteller), 95–98
Florida
    armchair expertise on
        teaching, 43–44
    book bans, 45
Florida Educational Leadership Exam
    (FELE), 9
Florida International University
    (FIU), 8, 11–12, 135, 147, 161
Florida Principal Leadership Standards
    (FPLS), 22
Floyd, George, 145
Focused Community Strategies (FCS)
    Urban Ministries, 136
"food desert," 50
food insecurity, higher education
    and, 98
For the Love of Books, Bazile
    (storyteller), 160–163
foster care system, 146–147, 165
Freire, Paulo, 32, 42, 136–137
Fremont High School, 173
From Adversity to Advocacy, Rodero
    (storyteller), 146–148
functionalist perspective
    Durkheim as father of, 48–49
    grounded leadership, 47–57
    societies and communities
        functioning, 47
fundraising, emergency dollars, 80

Gates, Bill, 116
Georgia, Atlanta cheating
    scandal, 118–119
Georgia Bureau of Investigation
    (GBI), 118
Georgia State University
    (GSU), 141–142
G.I. Bill, 52–53
giftedness
    child's worth, 13–14
    student's, 33, 92

glasses, student needing, 72
Golden Scholars program, 147
Goldrick-Rab, Sara, 106–107
    building teams and research, 109
    Fix Something Unfair? That's What
        I Do All Day (storyteller), 95–98
    former allies, 108–109
    nonacademic challenges of graduate
        student, 106–107
Graduate Record Exam
    (GRE), 141–142, 152
Gramsci, Antonio, 50
grit
    achievement and, 56
    Duckworth on, 71–72, 86
    Grit (Duckworth), 71–74 n.1
    "grit craze," 51–52
guardians, education partnering
    with, 25
Guttman Community
    College, 169–170

Hamilton-Wentworth
    District, 98–99, 100–101
handouts, 135–136, 151, 188*t*
hand-ups, 136, 151, 188*t*
    philosophy, 136
Harrington, Michael, 17–18
Harvard Graduate School of
    Education, 140–141
Harvard University, 111–112
Hattie, John, 67–68
Haveman, Robert, 19
Heritage High School, 145
hidden curriculum, 13
higher education, food insecurity
    and, 98
History Will Not Repeat Itself,
    Williamson, 127–131
holistic approach, Duncan on
    education, 139
honors track, Williamson with gifted
    Black girls, 128–131
hooks, bell, 30

Hoover Institution, 115
hope, 32
Hope Center for College, Community, and Justice, 97
HOPE program, 149
human condition, resilience of communities, 36
human dignity, action and change, 155–156
"Hungry, Homeless, and in College" (Goldrick-Rab et al), *New York Times*, 96
Hungry for Sight Words, Donors Choose project, 162
Hunter College, 170–171
Hurricane Sandy (superstorm), 79, 81, 85–86
Hypolite, Liane, 10

identity politics, 79
ideology
  formal definition, 47
  meritocracy, 50
I Have a Dream (IHAD), Chicago chapter, 138
imagery, stories, 27–28
Imposter Syndrome, 8–9
inclusion
  climate of, 11
  promoting, 106
inequality, race- and class-based, 14
Institute for Research on Race and Public Policy, 94
  Lewis, 91–94
institutions, social structures, 58
insurgent, mindset, 176
integration, 20
Integration Interrupted (Tyson), 13
intergenerational inequality, 58
International Community High School, South Bronx, 169
interventionist approach, Wolder's, 85
"Introduction to Educational Leadership," graduate-level course, 8

investigative approaches, overcoming structural barriers and obstacles, 90–91
invisible backpacks, 144, 153
Israeli citizens, October 7, 2023 massacre, 171
It Requires Naming It, Lewis (storyteller), 91–94
"It Was Possible to Do Both," Wolder (storyteller), 82–85
Ivy League, 102

Jan's Dream, Whitfield (storyteller), 143–146
Jim Crow laws, 14
Johnson College Prep, 149–150
joy, successful educational leadership, 176–177
JP Morgan Chase, 79
justice, prioritizing, 36
Juvenile Temporary Detention Center (JTDC), 55–56
Juwara, Bashir, Nothing to Lose (storyteller), 168–172

K-12 curriculum
  race in, 46
  rising costs in, 90
K-12 Education Koret Task Force, 115
Kadens, Pete, 137, 152–153
  Tailored Resources Are the Seeds That Spark Community Empowerment (storyteller), 148–151
Kadens Family Foundation, 148–151
Kardashian, Kim, 51
Keeping Track (Oakes), 13
Keepin' It Real (Carter), 103–104, 103–104 n.5
King, John B., Jr., 70, 89
  adopting high-expectations, high-support mindset, 87
  Safe, but Stretched (storyteller), 75–78
  as young orphan, 75, 85–86

knowledge, formalized curriculum, 48
knowledge acquisition
  life beyond school walls, 42
  schools for academic, 41–42

Ladson-Billings, Gloria, 19
leaders
  community assisting, 37–39
  equity-oriented, open to divergent thinking, 132–133
leadership
  community-engaged, 100
  earning credentials, 144
  perspectives informing grounded, 47–57
leadership research, challenging status quo, 57
leadership scholarship, 10
lead poisoning, 50–51
learning traffic, 137
Le-Reselosa, Jason, 111
Levine, Linda, 91, 109
Lewis, Amanda, 16–17, 20, 106, 108, 109
  It Requires Naming It (storyteller), 91–94
  University of California, Berkeley, 91–93
Liberation Schools, Black Panthers' Oakland-based, 172
literacy, books promoting, 160–163
Loewenstein, George, 88–89
London School of Economics, 167–168
Lupton, Robert, 136

McCall, Leslie, 53–54
McDonald's, 51–52
McGhee, Heather, 16
Malloy, John, 106, 110
  Closing Schools . . . Equitably (storyteller), 98–101
  community-minded research, 108

Maori Indigenous Schools, New Zealand, 173
marginalized communities, 12
  Rodero supporting, 152
Marx, Karl, 49–50
Matos Rodriguez, Felix, 171
Mead, George Herbert, 62–63
Mehta, Jal, 27
mental health, COVID-19 pandemic, 124–125
mentorship, 146–148
meritocracy
  creation of gaps, 51
  ideology of, 50
  principles of, 114
Miami-Dade Community College, 161
Miami-Dade public schools, 163
Michelangelo's masterpiece, David, 43
Midsummer Night's Dream (Shakespeare), 77
Mitra, Dana, 10, 24–25
Mok, Olivia, 134
  Asian Enough (storyteller), 124–127
  identity and voice, 133
Mother of All, The, Blanchette (storyteller), 163–165
movement, Goldrick-Rab, 96
MSNBC, 51–52
"Multiplication Is for White People" (Delpit), 141
Museum of Natural History, 77
Musk, Elon, 51
Muslim students, 170–171

narrative-based research, questions to answer, 21
narratives, importance of stories, 27–30
National Association for the Advancement of Colored People (NAACP), 157
Network for Public Education, 116

Newberg v. Board of Public Ed, 157–158
New Jersey Veterans Stand Down, 136
Newsweek (magazine), 116
New York City
  Asian American Student Advocacy Project (ASAP), 125–127
  Bloomberg's mission for schools, 122–123
  Department of Education, 121
  Department of Youth and Community Development, 168
New York Post (newspaper), 159
New York Times (newspaper), 77, 96
New York University (NYU), 78–81, 120
Nieves, Lisette, 176
  Obedience Will Only Get You So Far (storyteller), 165–168
No Child Left Behind (NCLB), 115, 117–118, 132
Noguera, Pedro, 28–29, 51–52, 61–62, 108, 133–134
  resignation, 132–133
  Stepping Down to Take a Stand (storyteller), 120–124
None of the Above (Robinson and Simonton), 117–120, 117–120 n.6, 134
Nothing to Lose, Juwara (storyteller), 168–172

Oakes, Jeannie, 13
Oakland Unified School District, 105, 109
Obama, Barack, 137, 168
Obedience Will Only Get You So Far, Nieves (storyteller), 165–168
Ogbu, John, 103–104, 106–107
O'Malley, Michael, 10
opportunity, 55–56
opportunity gap(s), 81
  books as, 59–61
opportunity hoarding, 15–16

oppositional culture theory, Ogbu, 103–104, 106–107
optimism
  educational leadership, 36
  hope and, 32
organizations, actors within social system, 49
Osterweil, Alan, 77–78, 87–88
others, 34–35
  being helped by, 33–35
Oxford, 71

parents, education partnering with, 25
Paying the Price (Goldrick-Rab), 95–98, 95–98 n.3
Perfect Storm and a Yellow Sweater, The, Anderson (storyteller), 78–81
pessimists, structuralists as, 59
Philadelphia Negro, The (Du Bois), 112
Phillips Brooks House Association, 75
play, kids and adults, 62–63
pools, public swimming, 16
"pornographic" label, Michelangelo's masterpiece, David, 43
Portela, Gabriella, 135
poverty, education and, 54
Poverty, by America (Desmond), 18
Power of Student Agency, The (Kundu), 33–34, 50, 63, 178–179
  story of "Rose" in, 33–34
principle, race as organizing principle, 93
privilege
  balance, 19
  defining, 18
  individual responsibility and, 54–55
problems of practice, students engaging with, 90–91
problem students, 84–85, 92

professional development, equity checklist, 85
Professional Standards for Educational Leaders (PSEL), 22
Professor of Educational Leadership, 11–12
Program for International Student Assessment (PISA) test, 52
Proud Boys, 14
proximate, offering high expectations and high support, 87–88
public education
  egalitarian ideology, 54
  framing, 179–180
  war against, 178
public schools
  charter and, 121–122
  desegregation, 127–128
  war against "woke," 31
public service, devotion to, 77
"pulse check" survey, 73–74

Race in the Schoolyard (Lewis), 93, 93 n.1
race relations, Du Bois, 113
racial equity, educational leaders, 94
racism, 14–15, 93
  modern form of, 133
  publish swimming pools, 16
  structural, 129
  systemic, 145
radical, 181–182
Ravitch, Diane, 118, 132
  Soul Searching (storyteller), 113–117
#RealCollege campaign, 96–97
"rebellious," framework, 53
recidivism rate, detention center, 55
Reducing and Removing Barriers to Make Way for Capable People, Delpit (storyteller), 140–143
Reign of Error (Ravitch), 113–114
research literature, 10
resilience, 151

achievement and, 56
Du Bois, 111–113
human condition, 36
revolutionary, 181
Rhodes Scholar, University of Oxford, 167–168
Robinson, Shani
  cheating scandal, 118–119
  None of the Above, 134
  restoring reputation, 133
  Wrongly Convicted and yet Unwavering in Conviction (storyteller), 117–120
Rodero, Jacqueline, 137, 152–153
  From Adversity to Advocacy (storyteller), 146–148

Safe, but Stretched, King (storyteller), 75–78
Sandlin, Jennifer, 10
Sarah and Joseph Jr. Dowling Professor of Sociology, Carter, 101–106
Saving Starfish, Duckworth (storyteller), 71–74
Schenck, Lillian, 183 *See also* Educational Leadership for Equity Toolkit
scholarship program, 150
schools
  academic knowledge, 41–42
  choice, 179
  closure process, 100
  definition, 41–42
  ever-unequal contexts of, 12–19
  Freire's work, 42
  social structures and social fabric, 58–59
  society and, 69
  symbiotic relationship with community, 43
  teacher demographics, 26
  Twain on, 42
school-to-prison pipeline (STPP), proliferation of, 49

Scott High School, 149
"seeing is believing," 29
segregation, 14
  affluence, 15–16
self, Mead on, as process, 62–63
self-control, achievement and, 56
self-improvement, pursuit of, 11
separate but equal, principle of, 14
servant leadership, 38
sexism, 14–15
Shields, Carolyn, 10, 57
Simonton, Anna, 119, 134
Simon Youth Academy
  (SYA), 163–165
Slovic, Paul, 88–89
Small, Deborah, 88–89
social capital, 63
  agency of students, 69
  definition, 63
  storytellers, 65
social cohesion, 48–50
socialization, capital and, 63
social justice
  activism and, 127
  experience drawing into
    activism, 166–168
social order, students and, 54
social production theory, 69
social reproduction theory, 52
social structures, institutions, 58
social welfare, community-based
  bonds, 152–153
society
  education in, 54
  schools and, 69
sociology, 58
  Du Bois as father of
    American, 111–112
  The Sociology of Leading Systems
    Change, 183*t*
Soul Searching, Ravitch
  (storyteller), 113–117
stakeholder buy-in, 11
stakeholders, 12

Stanford University, 115
Stanley, Darrius, 10
State of New York on Performance
  Standards Consortium, 159
State University of New York
  (SUNY), 75–78, 120–121, 123,
  133–134
status quo, disrupting and
  challenging, 57
Stepping Down to Take a Stand,
  Noguera (storyteller), 120–124
Step to College, 172
Stick to Your Guns (Le-Reselosa), 111
stories, importance of, 27–30
storyteller(s), 39–40
  Anderson, Noel S., 78–81
  Bazile, Debra, 160–163
  Blanchette, Jennifer, 163–165
  Carter, Prudence, 101–106
  Delpit, Lisa, 140–143
  diverse, 24–27
  Duckworth, Angela, 71–74
  Duncan, Arne, 137–139
  Duncan-Andrade, Jeffrey, 172–175
  Fine, Michelle, 156–160
  Goldrick-Rab, Sara, 95–98
  Juwara, Bashir, 168–172
  Kadens, Pete, 148–151
  King, John B., Jr., 75–78
  Lewis, Amanda, 91–94
  Malloy, John, 98–101
  Mok, Olivia, 124–127
  Nieves, Lisette, 165–168
  Noguera, Pedro, 120–124
  Ravitch, Diane, 113–117
  Robinson, Shani, 117–120
  Rodero, Jacqueline, 146–148
  Whitfield, James, 143–146
  Williamson, Denise, 127–131
  Wolder, Sharon, 82–85
storytelling, 88–89, 186*t*, 188*t*, 189*t*
structuralist perspective, educational
  leaders, 59
structural racism, 129

structure-agency dichotomy, kindergarten classroom library, 58–62
student(s)
  achievement and well-being for all, 30–32
  jitteriness of, 50
  relationship of teachers with, 164–165
  school drop-off, 174
  social order, 54
  support for, 97
  testing, 142
student enrollment
  administration and, 100–101
  Hamilton-Wentworth, 98–99
student-entered agenda, honesty, 100
students of color, expectations, 20
Sue Duncan Children's Center, Chicago, 138
Sum of Us, The (McGhee), 16
systemic racism, 145, 178–179

Tailored Resources Are the Seeds That Spark Community Empowerment, Kadens (storyteller), 148–151
teachers, determination of, 120
Teachers College, Columbia University, 116
Teach for America (TFA), 117
Teaching When the World Is on Fire (Delpit), 141
TED Talk (2020), 55
Temple University, 97
Testifying for Good, Fine (storyteller), 156–160
testing, students, 142
There's Room at the Table for All of Us, Carter (storyteller), 101–106
Tinker vs. Des Moines Independent Community School District (1969), 48

Title I, 179
Title I high schools, 28–29
toolkit. *See* Educational Leadership for Equity Toolkit
Toronto District School Board, 98
Truman Scholarship, 167–168
Trump, Donald, 124
Twain, Mark, 42
Twitter account, "Old Diane Ravitch," 115
Tyson, Karolyn, 13

underprivilege, defining, 18
Unified Children's Court (UCC), 147–148
United States, class and race, 52–53
University of California, Berkeley, 91–93, 105, 172
University of Chicago, 54, 138
University of Illinois Chicago, 91–94
University of Oxford, 167–168
University of Pennsylvania, 71–74, 112, 157–158
University of Southern California, 120–124
University of Texas Permian Basin, 143
University of Toledo, 148–149
University of Wisconsin-Milwaukee, 95
upstream effects, 50–51
Urban Education Semester program, 91
US Berkeley School of Education, 101–102
US Interagency Council on Homelessness, 76–77
US Secretary of Education
  Duncan, 138–139
  King, 75–78

values, education, 156
Villaraigosa, Antonio (Mayor), 159
Viral Justice (Benjamin), 31–32

visionary leadership, 34
vocabulary, textbooks building, 83

Warren, Earl (Chief Justice), 14
We Have to Look Out for Each Other, Duncan (storyteller), 137–139
welfare queens, 17–18
well-being, importance for all, 30–32
wellness, understanding and tending to children's, 173–174
White House Initiative on Educational Excellence for Hispanics, 168
White Space, Black Hood (Cashin), 15
white supremacy, 14
  term, 178–179
Whitfield, James, 137, 153
  Jan's Dream (storyteller), 143–146
Whitfield, Jan, 143, 146
Williamson, Denise, 11–12, 25, 46, 55–56, 134, 182

academically gifted Black girls (Nicole and Christina), 128–131
History Will *Not* Repeat Itself (storyteller), 127–131
Williamson, Diane, 133
Wisconsin, student survey, 95–96
witnessing, 31–32
"woke," war against, 31
Wolder, Sharon, 70
  AP European history, 86
  "It Was Possible to Do Both" (storyteller) 82–85
world history class, Wolder, 82
World War II, 156
Wrongly Convicted and yet Unwavering in Conviction, Robinson (storyteller), 117–120

Yankee Stadium, 64
Year Up New York (YU NY), Anderson, 78–81, 88